L.A. STORIES:
THE VOICES OF CULTURAL DIVERSITY

L.A. STORIES:
THE VOICES OF CULTURAL DIVERSITY

CAROL CLARK OTTESEN

Intercultural Press, Inc.

For information, contact:
Intercultural Press, Inc.
P.O. Box 700
Yarmouth, Maine 04096 USA

Book design and production by Patty J. Topel
Cover design by Ralph Copeland

Printed in the United States of America.

98 97 96 95 94   1 2 3 4 5

Library of Congress Cataloging-in-Publication Data

L.A. stories: the voices of cultural diversity/[compiled by]
   Carol Clark Ottesen.
      p.   cm.
   ISBN 1-877864-26-9
   1. Minorities—California—Los Angeles—Literary collec-
tions. 2. American literature—California—Los Angeles. 3.
American literature—Minority authors. 4. American literature—20th century. I. Ottesen, Carol Clark. II. Title: L.A. stories. III. Title: Los Angeles stories.

PS572.L6L3 1993
810.8'0920693—dc00   93-36926
                                              CIP

Dedicated to Sterling, who, in the words of my oldest son, is "a rock you can climb onto in the middle of the ocean," and to my children, Eric, Craig, Lisa, Susan and Robin, who asked me to tell these stories.

Acknowledgments

Without the willingness of my students to write with candor, authenticity and courage, this compilation would not be possible. I thank them for giving me a fresh perspective which would be difficult to obtain in any other way.

I acknowledge the encouragement of Dr. David Heifetz of California State University, Dominguez Hills, in the initial stages of the manuscript and appreciate his continuing good-humored support. Chris McCarthy, Dean of Academics of Los Angeles Harbor College, and President James L. Heinselman of Harbor College also read the manuscript and expressed their support and encouragement. June B. Smith of the English Department at Harbor College and June Schwarzmann of CSUDH also provided many helpful suggestions. Thanks to Roy Anthony Shabla for giving me his insights, both poetic and practical. Especially I wish to express my love and appreciation to my daughter, Robin Phillips and her husband Jerry, owners of Ultratype, Inc., for their untiring assistance in the preparation of the manuscript. And, of course, I express my gratitude to a patient, graciously critical editor, David S. Hoopes, whose life's work testifies to the notion that we are all related.

Table of Contents

4—L.A. on Fire 67

5—A Richer Stew 85

6—Conflict in the Dark Room 101

At the conclusion of the pipe ceremonies of the Plains Indians the participants murmur: "We are all related." It is desirable then, for our societal structures to be bold and large enough to affirm rather than deny. The tribal relationship of Indians is therefore never based upon the tolerance of others but the experience of self as part of others. *We are all related.*

—Jamake Highwater
The Primal Mind

Introduction

New Ellis Island

Los Angeles has been dubbed "The World State" and "The New Ellis Island" because of the vast number of different racial and ethnic groups living here. Nearly one in two new residents of the Los Angeles area is a recent immigrant.

Latinos, blacks, and Asian Americans make up about 59 percent of the population.

In the Los Angeles County schools, Latinos, Asians, blacks, American Indians, and Pacific Islanders account for 74 percent of the student population.

In the Los Angeles Unified School District, 82 languages are now being spoken.

No one knows exactly what the coming of this strikingly pluralistic Los Angeles means, but racial tension is palpable and has become increasingly violent. Gangs that fifteen or twenty years ago fought only with fists or sometimes knives are now armed with automatic weapons to protect turf. Blacks and Koreans are at a standoff, marked by open violence. The Japanese at the start of the semester in my class do not talk to Koreans. A tall, stocky black man in my class notices that white women are "scared" around him. A Kurdish professor is refused housing "because she has an accent." Anti-Semitic slogans are scrawled on the door of a West Los Angeles synagogue. The burned-out city blocks of the May, 1992, riots still scar the face of the city.

I would like to believe that heterogeneous America will meld into a "cosmic race," as José Vasconcelos envisioned in his 1920s book by that name, but I think it is impossible for individuals to extricate themselves from the tangle of their cultural experience, from the long roots that bear them up. Contemporary technology can combine all the sounds of different musical instruments into one electronic keyboard, but what results is not the same as hearing the separate instruments joined together in a magnificent orchestra. Utopia seems to lie in infinite variety and the moving together in concert. To say we have a long way to go is an understatement.

What can be done? Both the answers and the questions are complex. Education is a frequently mentioned solution, but a general one. Merely preparing the student for vocational success will not directly address the problem as effectively as an education which examines values, morals, and ethics, and an education which implements cooperative learning and sharing.

David Rieff, in an article in the *Los Angeles Times*, quotes Linda Wong, Director of California Tomorrow:

> California—eventually the nation, if the demographic predictions are correct—is a lifeboat. If the boat is springing leaks because of inadequate and poor-quality education, because of deepening poverty...the people who are sitting in the boat are going to figure out some way of plugging those leaks and working together if they value their lives.

Ultimately, all we have are words. I see multicultural groups coming together in the classroom and sharing their deepest concerns as a beginning. These groups can be fostered by any sponsor—religious, political, educational, or social. Caught in a vicious down-spiral of poverty, lack of education and self-esteem, and the need to belong to a "family," these children of ghettos and barrios will become social dependents unless quality education and alternative ways of being are made available. Then, as these cultures come together in the classroom, we drop the "naming" and see one another simply as human beings.

In Native-American cultures, the well-being of the individual lies in the quality of his or her relationship to others; in fact, a tribal member can only prefigure the self as standing in relationship to the group. A remarkable similarity occurs also among tribal peoples on other continents where "the relatedness of the individual and the tribe extends outward beyond the family, band, or clan to include all things of the world. Thus nothing exists in isolation" (Highwater 1981, 172).

A statement by a young man of Maori descent concerned about American adoration of individuality makes the same point. "I believe that I am an individual, but not totally, as I can never separate myself from my relationship to a family, a community, the earth and God. I can't give up the Polynesian attitude that if everyone else can't rise with me, it is not worth rising at all."

Delores Huff in her essay "The Tribal Ethic, The Protestant Ethic and Economic Development" presents intrinsic differences and then argues "that development can take place that is congruent with the culture, rather than changing the culture in order to attain development....Individuals may assimilate, but tribal societies do not....Tribal societies either emerge collectively out of poverty or remain collectively in poverty."

Again, we rise together, or not at all. And "together" allows for discrete cultural groups, each aware of the impulse toward ethnocentricity, each honoring, if not celebrating the differences. Even Ralph Waldo Emerson, the premier voice of American individualism, points out the constant tension in man and nature between unity and variety. Likewise, psychologist/philosopher Carl Jung has aptly said, "We all finally unite in one family tree, but what is a tree without its elaborately dissimilar branches?"

In the geographical smallness of the classroom, through discussion and sharing of strong feelings, I see understanding begin to dawn. And even then it is not a merging, not a loss of personal identity, but a clearer ordering of individual and group identity. Writing is an exercise in self-knowledge, and the sharing of that writing is learning to become a citizen of the world. Multicultural studies encourage us to look at traditionally excluded cultures and study them on their own terms rather than through the eyes of the dominant culture. And we cannot learn about differences without discovering our alikeness.

Yet the very term "ethnic diversity" implies the perception of "we" and "they." Thus, tolerance would seem to be the primary requirement in the attempt to live together in a culturally pluralistic society. But merely putting up with or being passively tolerant will not solve our conflicts. Until we establish a relatedness, a universal "we," a realization that in our veins runs common blood and that a blow to humankind is a blow to our own bodies, we cannot live together in peace.

Cats in a Bag?

Walt Whitman, nineteenth-century poet/spokesman for American democracy, heard America singing many individual themes, "Each singing what belongs to him or her and to none else....Singing...their strong melodious songs." Harmony is not mentioned; the ear hears a counterpoint of simultaneous melodies, moving in a pattern of dissonance and resolution. But even Whitman could not foresee the cacophony of today, this vast mosaic of multiethnicity that has changed the face of America. The ensuing problems of this change might tempt us to compose a new American song: "Cats in a Bag."

Yet Whitman acknowledged his own idealism and, in the presentation of the vision for American democracy, delineated the reality. Though Whitman was mesmerized by the Emersonian idea of individualism, he was acutely aware of the whole and the need for unity. In his poem "Kosmos," Whitman identifies the ideal maker of a democratic world as one "Who includes diversity...who, constructing the house of himself or herself, sees races, eras, generations...dwelling there...inseparable together."

But the looming paradox of the coexistence of unity and diversity keeps us in a "cradle endlessly rocking." The pull between self-identification and group acceptance and the wish for a world in a state of tranquil repose—yet a world of energy and freedom—creates a tension sometimes beyond control.

This book documents the possibilities for understanding each other and the need for recognition of this changing face of America. The multiethnic classroom, which could be a microcosmic model of Los Angeles, of the United States, or even of the world, is a place to begin.

Voices

One's-self I sing, a simple separate person,
Yet utter the word Democratic, the word, En-Masse.

—Walt Whitman
"One's-Self I Sing"

As an instructor at Los Angeles Harbor College and California State University, Dominguez Hills, I enter a world of color and diversity—a culturally pluralistic world of infinite variety.

The demographic makeup at Cal State Dominguez is approximately 34 percent black, 14 percent Hispanic, 47 percent white, the remainder a mix of Asians and Pacific Islanders, and approximately three hundred international students on student visas. Here I teach in the Interdisciplinary Studies Department, both in American Studies and Writing Adjunct, a lecture/tutorial program in which the instructor monitors the writing of research papers in other disciplines. The unique structure of this program allows me to become well acquainted with students, not only through their writing but also through one-on-one, twenty-minute sessions each week.

The demographics at Los Angeles Harbor College are slightly different, but nonetheless diverse: 28 percent Hispanic, 14 percent black, 7 percent Asian, 11 percent Pacific Islander, and 37 percent white. Students report twenty-one different ethnicities. Here I teach remedial English for those who have failed to meet the requirements for Freshman English and, therefore, I have many students for whom English is a second language. This preparatory class calls for writing essays, many of them personal narratives, and I become privy to special corners of these students' lives, if not the interiors. They document life in the inner city and the struggle to escape its attendant problems. Many of my students are bicultural American citizens, immigrants, or international students. As I read their work I am fascinated, incredulous, angry, disappointed, sometimes bored, but most often informed and enriched.

The following are excerpts from some of these student essays, reproduced as they were written, with the addition of my own editorial comments to give context and continuity. From my first semester of teaching, I have felt some of these essays deserved wider readership. I wanted others to hear these voices from a rich but sometimes misunderstood world. Most of this work is, with student permission, from a small publication we produce each semester; however, I have changed or altered the names where I felt it to be appropriate.

Included also is documentation of my own cultural experience as a white observer of this encounter. The point here is not to sensationalize, sentimentalize, ridicule, or blame, but to share the sound of these voices that document what it is to be human.

The Gossamer Thread

Noon, September 19, 1989. *Fall semester, my first class at Los Angeles Harbor College. Twenty-five students, mostly Hispanic, some blacks, a few Asians, and maybe four Caucasians, are crowded into a hot barrackslike classroom. I am more excited than nervous, and my face is flushed from the heat. My students seem inordinately quiet, unlike my classes at the university where they are older and more interactive. These students seem passive, distant, deferent, and I wonder if I can jump over this huge abyss of differences in culture, age, and economic strata that divides us.*

On the way home in the car I recall my own cultural milieu. Though I was raised in Washington, D.C. and have had five American Indian foster children, I wonder about all the unverbalized baggage I bring to this experience. I am hoping, like Whitman's noiseless patient spider, to connect—"Till the bridge you will need be form'd....Till the gossamer thread you fling catch somewhere...."

1
The Encounter

I know there are many people who, as dogs always bark at strangers, so also often condemn and hate what they do not understand.

—Pico della Mirandola (1463-1494)
The Dignity of Man

From the Border to the Barrio

Harbor College, 1989. *Eighteen-year-old Lucia Cervantes is stoic, disdainful in a way that almost distracts from her beauty. She seems older, streetwise, almost dares me to teach her. The sensitivity of her first essay surprises me.*

The Christmas I remember most is the Christmas Eve we came to the United States. We hadn't seen my Dad for three years because he had been working up here and we stayed in Mexico. One day my Dad sent a letter saying he would send someone to get us over the border and that he would wait on the other side for us. We started on our journey, walking to catch the bus to meet a man we had never seen in our lives.

My Dad wanted us to come on Christmas because he knew there would be less cops watching the border. It was very, very cold and someone had stolen our jackets and we had no food. My mom told us that as soon as we crossed that line we would be with our dad and be happy and warm. That thought kept me warm, but my little sister was only one year old and was very cold. We worried about her crying and making noise. When we crossed the border we were in a dirty alley and a dog kept barking, so that man hid us in a trash can. We slept there in the trash cans until about midnight. My brother covered my little sister with his coat.

Finally the man came back and led us through. My father was waiting on the other side with some jackets and warm food. That was my first Christmas in the United States. Though I can never forget that cold winter night, for us it was a great Christmas to be together after three years.

Lucia now lives in a barrio in Los Angeles. She tells me in an interview that her father cannot work because of an indus-

3

trial accident. She and her mother and sisters work to support the family and her brother is in jail. She writes in another essay:

Some have beautiful teenage experiences, but I have spent much of my time in hospitals, jails and funerals because of gang violence. My brother was stabbed as he sat beside me in a car. I don't know how to stop all this pain. No one ever forgives. Sometimes at night I hear the chopper in the air, the roaring sound of a police car and the crying of an ambulance and I wonder if it's someone I know....People talk and write books but they don't know the pain.

Lucia writes a poem "La Raza" at the end of her paper on gang violence:

Written In Memory of:

Mark	16 years old	Magella	15 years old
Ditto	18 years old	Shorty	15 years old

> Dare if you can
> to share through our eyes
> to find lost dreams
> within darkened skies . . .
>
> Dare if you will
> to challenge hell's fires,
> to recapture the sunrise
> with life's passions, desires . . .
>
> Dare if we can
> to touch each other
> as Raza we stand
> Sister and Brother.

The last day of school she puts a fluffy, white stuffed cat with a pink ribbon on my desk. A note written on purple notepaper says "Thanks."

Mi Memry

Miguel Garcia is presently a gang member who came over the border from Guadalajara at age thirteen, alone. He lives with an uncle who is disabled, and his aunt takes in children to support the family. He walks five miles to school and saves money for a bicycle by working at a fast-food restaurant. He is illiterate, charming, polite, and eager to learn, and though he is twenty-one he looks like a fourteen-year-old. Miguel has been taking drugs since he was a child, but says he's drug-free now. He limps with a leg wound from a drive-by shooting. His first writing sample:

I lov mi mother. Becus I not see her por a long tim. She is stil aliv? I thing so but my hart hurt. This is mi memry.

I talk to him about the Learning Assistance Center and taking a remedial class. He has had the remedial class, he says. He wants to stay in this class.

"I will study a lot. Give me extra work. I have to stay home all the time because I can't go out on the street anymore. See, I was standing on the corner and these guys drive by and shoot me in the leg, and kill my friend standing next to me. When I was in the hospital I say no more going around with those guys. So when I quit hanging around, these guys in my own gang get mad. They say to me, 'Hey, Chico, watch your back.' So I watch my back. I just go to work, go to school and stay locked in my room at night. So now I can practice writing and get good."

I accept his promise but I know he will not pass. He comes faithfully. He good-naturedly enters the class discussions and seems to be trying hard. I meet with him to go over his extra work and give him a ride home several times because he has to walk so far.

"Thank you, Miss Carol. Very nice for the ride." *At least ten kids greet him at the gate, hugging his legs and smiling as if he were a hero.*

One week he does not come to class. Another week passes and I call. The number has been disconnected. I don't see him again.

Solomonsville, Arizona, 1935. *My father, principal and teacher at the school in this small desert town, surveys his first class—mostly Mexican and American Indian, a few whites, most of them without shoes. Father takes me to class and stands me on the desk to sing, "Animal Crackers in My Soup."*

After class, a skinny Mexican boy waits for him patiently until everyone is gone. Then asks plaintively, "I got a hungry. You got a biscuit?"

My father gives him a nickel and he skips away. I pelt my father with questions. "Why does he talk funny?" "Why is he hungry?" "Why doesn't he have shoes on?" "Why is he poor?" "Where does he live?" We walk home together in the dusty streets, hand in hand, my Japanese parasol as shelter from the sun, and I feel different and "other." We pass the Mexican houses and I am curious but not remorseful. I think I am poor too because my mother cut a cardboard sole to put in my shoe that morning because it had a hole. I swim with my Mexican neighbors in the irrigation ditch, we share the horned toads we find in the rocks, and I forget about inequities.

Conchita, our housekeeper, is a mix of Mexican, Apache, and Pima. One day she takes me to her dirt-floored adobe house and I watch her make tortillas. She pats them flat on her brown thigh and sets them to sizzle on the wood stove. I eat them hot with honey, and the sweet honey melts down my elbow.

Conchita is crying as she talks to my mother. Her sister's newborn baby is dying because she has no breast milk and they cannot afford to buy milk, nor do they have a place to keep it fresh. My mother is nursing my sister, and she offers to nurse Conchita's sister's baby also.

Conchita brings the baby several times a day. Sometimes both drink at once, blond baby on one breast, black-haired baby on the other. Mother asks me to tell no one about this or she will be criticized. I wonder why, and I do not tell because this seems sacred and mysterious.

Being Poor

Claudia Gonzalez comes to my office after the first day of class, somewhat distraught because her husband opposes her going back to school. He has refused to supervise the three children during her one English class, and she does not know if she can continue. She will try to get her husband's aunt to watch the children. Claudia makes arrangements and continues the class. After several one-on-one sessions with me, she writes this paper:

I came from a big family of six girls and two boys. We lived in Mexico and were very poor at the time, and I could not understand that being poor is nothing to be ashamed of.

Although I was poor, I used to hang around with the more popular and rich people. I never put myself down in front of them. But I did feel inferior and I was too proud to let them know my true feelings.

In a way, I can say that I was popular too. I used to be good in sports and academically. If I was not the first, at least I would be the second or third. But still I would be ashamed for not having all the money my "friends" had for lunch or have the new clothes they want.

I worked very hard to understand that being poor was nothing to be ashamed of. My husband is Mexican-American and is not rich but he has a better economic position and a "good name" as we say in my country. But the feeling has come back more strongly.

My "new family" thinks I am not good enough for my husband because my father did not marry my mother and I was so poor. But I am not going to feel sorry for myself or my mother. I realize that being poor is nothing bad; on the contrary, it makes you stronger. I think everyone is equal no matter how much money they have. I suppose I think this way because I have been poor. Perhaps if I ever graduate and become a doctor, then, God willing, perhaps I will never have the feeling of being poor again.

My mother always said that money changes people's feelings. That's why I wonder if I ever want to have money. I just want enough to have my children's future secure.

Claudia finds a job as a housekeeper in the evenings and takes two of her children with her. She is as diligent as her time allows her to be but barely meets the requirements for a C in the class. She cries when she finds out she has passed the class and is still eligible for financial aid.

My Cardboard House

Erlinda Loriega's feet do not touch the floor as she sits in the first row. She is a delicate Asian beauty as tiny as a ten-year-old, this student who came from the Philippines about four years ago. She is painfully shy and never speaks up in class, but sits primly with a permanent smile. She writes:

Back in Manila, where I grew up, my family was very poor. We lived in a very bad house, partly cardboard. My father was an industrious salesman who tried desperately to make enough commission for Christmas because we had no money.

On Christmas eve, my father finally got a commission, and he took the bus home from work and seated himself at the back. A man beside him asked for a match for his cigarette. My father reached in his pocket for the match but instead out came his money in an envelope. The money scattered all over and as he tried to pick it up, two men stopped him. They told my father they wanted his money. My father refused. But the bus was crowded and no one cared what was going on. Everyone was afraid, even the bus driver. Those men took all my father's money and beat him up. He thought he could beat those two skinny men in a fight but they have gangs on the bus and they beat my father like a boxing bag.

It was amazing that my father was able to get home. His face was badly bruised, his ribs cracked and he couldn't work for six months.

The next day was Christmas. That year we had nothing. We settled down with hot coffee and bread. And it was all right because we cared more about taking care of my father. We closed down our door the whole day so the neighbors wouldn't suspect anything. We were also scared. That night about ten o'clock, there was a knock on the door. My mother hesitated to open it but the knock persisted and my Mom opened it. There was a man who knew my dad. He gave my mom fifty pesos for his debt with my dad. Right away, my mom left for the open market to buy us food. We said our prayers in thankfulness. The great significance of this was the hope it gave us. I truly believe there's hope everywhere, especially now that I am here in the land of the free and bountiful.

My Eyes Are Falling Down

*Limnghe Huygh is Chinese, raised in Vietnam, a young
mother of two children and the wife of an older Vietnamese
husband. She is a college graduate in her country and has
come back to school to improve her English. Her husband
emigrated some time before she did, but she was caught in
the net of the war, unable to join him. Her wealthy parents
paid for her escape to the United States in a small boat, a
trip she describes as most difficult and dangerous. "I thought
I might die," she said.*

*But she is glad she came and happy except that her husband
"make her work too much" and "tell me mostly I am dumb."
She says she must pass the writing exam and will do whatever she has to. She comes twice a week for tutorials and
doubles up on her hours at the Learning Assistance Center. I
don't have much hope she will pass though I do note her
diligence and determination.*

*After she leaves my office, I write about this pull between
innocence and experience, formality and spontaneity:*

> Lightly you flutter into my room
> a garden butterfly blown through the window
> by mistake,
> settling on the chair before me,
> your color flashing and catching
> against the dry gray walls
>
> so loudly I cannot hear
> you stumble over verbs
> and shatter sentences;
> they are like the random color of your wings
> I am loathe to order
>
> But studying you do until
> you say *your eyes are falling down.*

Do I mark these words with red
when here I stand in academic grays,
stunned and reeling
at the blazing color of your innocence?

*I ask all the students to keep journals and then I collect
them for reading and grading at the end of the course. She
writes in her journal:*

...Every Tuesday and Thursday I meet my English teacher at
her office. She has given me an encouragement for my
learning ability. Every time I talk to her I feel happy as I can
be a bird. I feel that nothing can hold me back and I am not
that dummy as I thought. I know I still have a long way to
learn to be what I want to be. But maybe I won't fail again.

*Early in the semester Limnghe translates a letter she has
written to her mother in Vietnam and asks me to review it to
see how she is doing in English.*

Oct. 12, 1986
To my beautiful mother:

I am so happy to read your own writing in your letter. I feel
very close to you. My heart squizzed and my tear came out
while I was reading each word from you. I miss you and
love you so much. I can't believe the life in Viet Nam is so
hard to live. There are so many people still want to get out
of there. Mom, I wish one day you could come here to stay
with me. Do you know that everyday before I go to work I
light one incense stick to pray for your health and I pray for
our union? I wait and wait, but my wish hasn't come true
yet. Almost eleven year have passed by so fast. I am so
sorry I can't be next to you to take care of you in your late age.

Your grandsons are very well behaved. I tell story about
you all the time. Your oldest grandson, he asked his uncle
not to buying a gift for him but to give him the money, so
he could send to you . . .

*Limnghe takes the qualifying exam at the semester's end
and passes.*

My First Impressions of U.S.A.

Harbor College, October 1991. *Sergio Gonzalez, a tall, fair Hispanic, called by one girl in the class "a real stud," comes to me after class and asks, in heavily accented English, if he can write on a subject other than nuclear weapons. "Too hard for me," he says. So I suggest he write about his first impressions of the United States, since earlier he told me he emigrated from Mexico only two years before. He composes the following essay:*

I used to hear my neighbors in Mexico saying, "If we were living in the U.S.A., we will be living better." At first, I didn't put too much attention on that until I heard some of the guys of my age saying the same, that here was cleaner and, in general, better. So after, I felt confident to find it out myself. So when my mother died, I thought I would go to U.S.A., even if my father didn't like it.

I got here at night. My brother picked me up and while he drove, I was watching the view from the car window and it seemed to be the truth. So I got impressed because in my old country not every place was that clean and that green color in the yard.

I slept that night thinking what it would look like on the outside of the house. So I woke up the next morning and found out the structure of houses are so different. In every house there was more than one car and I could only see few people on the streets.

I was surprised when I found out about all the public service that people have here. The cities are well-organized. Children are able to go to school on buses. The laws are strict so anybody who breaks them will have punishment. But also I had bad impressions too. Many people abuse drugs and gang violence turns out to be a serious problem.

14

I got a job in a restaurant. I walked in and said, "Good Morning." The manager said, "Sergio, pick up the plates on Table 12." "Yes," I responded, finding my way to the kitchen to ask a man who speaks my language to ask what the manager said. After a few weeks of having the problem of not understanding, I started to know what people were saying. But it was hard and I felt stupid.

The biggest impression was that even if you are in a place where there are many people, they don't talk to each other. It looked to me like everybody was in his own thoughts and not aware of others. Of course, in my country, it's not the same. We say hello to everyone, even strangers.

But I think all this happens to all people that emigrate to a foreign country and it takes time to adapt to that way of life.

Sergio barely passes the exit writing exam but he has cer-tainly begun to adapt. By the end of the semester he is wearing surfer shorts, conversing freely with a couple of very interested girls, and shows me some promotional pic-tures of himself that he is using to get a job as a male model.

Crossing the Border

December 1989. *I write a poem, a song for all the Lucias I have known.*

The boys do not breathe when she walks in class
their eyes move slowly sidelong as she sits
like a cat folding and settling at her desk
caramel legs beneath a short skirt, slit.
her dusky eyes like painted asterisks,
surprised by lips blood-red and exquisite.

She stands, begins to read how she came here:
"We hid inside a trash can all that night;
my coat was stolen and I couldn't cry
I swallowed tears and shook with cold and fright
then at the sign, I ran from the dark moon
into my father's arms hugging me tight.

"Now we live together in the barrio;
but when it's night we lie low in our beds
because of gunfire through the window, then
when I hear sirens, thoughts come in my head
like knives that flash and catch in someone's gut
a homeboy rides away wounded or dead.

"Right now my father cannot work at all;
his foot was nearly cut off at the plant
my mother takes in little kids to tend
my brother worked but he's in jail and can't.
people write books but they don't know this place
you learn quick or you die without a chance.

"Sometimes I think God hides from all of us
yet one day through the early morning rays
of sun through stained glass windows at the church
I felt him smiling on my dreams; I said
Raza. La Raza rise." (A small bell rings;
her voice shivers and echoes down the day):

"Dare if you will to find forgotten dreams
To recapture sunrise with desire
Dare if we will to reach and touch each other
As Raza we stand, sister and brother."
No one moves as she walks to her chair,
the noonday sun striking her hair with fire.

2
Surviving

In our wish to survive physically, we obey the biological impulse imprinted on us since birth of living substance and transmitted by millions of years of revolution. The wish to be alive "beyond survivial" is the creation of man in history, his alternative to despair and failure.

—Erich Fromm
The Revolution of Hope

Washington, D.C., 1940. *Blacks in the back of the bus only. Blacks expected to cross the street rather than pass me on the sidewalk. A black boy dances on the corner of 16th and Columbus Avenue for coins. A black man shines my father's shoes at the corner newspaper stand. A black girl spits on me while I am on the monkey bars at the park for no obvious reason. I cry alone because I do not understand and think I have done something wrong.*

Suzi, the "colored lady" who comes in to take care of us children while my mother types my father's doctoral dissertation leaves and never comes back after my little brother asks her why some people call them "niggers." I ask my mother why. She shrugs and is strangely quiet.

"What makes people black anyway?" I ask.

"God. He makes flowers and people in all colors."

I am wondering if there are purple and green people somewhere I don't know about.

Later, at the Lincoln Memorial, my father picks me up when no one is looking and puts me on Lincoln's massive marble knee. I touch the bigness and feel sheltered, and in that moment, I do not doubt that if Lincoln believed it, certainly all men are created equal.

My Life Is Boring

A black woman about forty, dressed in a worn yellow sweat suit, ambles into my office and plunks into the chair beside my desk with a sigh. She has almost-orange corn braids, two inches of gray at the roots and a passive face. She is saying she must write a twenty-five-page autobiography for her Historical Perspectives class, but she can't think of anything to write.

"My life is boring," *she says.*

"What do you do?" I venture.

LaWanda's shoulders shrug. "I have three kids. I work. Word processing."

She looks out the window and wants to be somewhere else. "Why would anybody want to read about my life?"

I look at the scratches in her notebook where she is writing her rough draft.

I was born in a little town in Georgia. We were poor and I didn't know my mother very well. She went away to work and I went to live with my grandmother.

"It's nothing much," *she says.* "Pretty ordinary."

We talk. My next student doesn't show, and in the next half hour her childhood unfolds.

"It isn't worth talking about. I lived in a shantytown, so poor I'm not going to tell you about it. Thirteen kids. I was in the middle." *LaWanda sighs again.* "Nothing more, really. I did leave, though, when I was thirteen." *Pause. I wait.*

Her story is hard in coming.

"Had to. I saw what I'd have to do. All my other sisters, well, my grandma gave them to white men for money. She came to get me one day when I was thirteen. Had a man for me in the barn. She nearly caught me but I got away. She ripped my dress, but I started running and I never came back. No matter what, I wasn't about to do that. No way. I got a job working for folks and then I hitched a ride to California.

"I knew my daddy was there and I wanted to see him. But I found he didn't want anything to do with me. I got a job working in a motel and met Leroy. First time anybody showed me any attention.

"Then we had this retarded daughter. She's both mentally and physically handicapped. And then had two more kids real quick. He couldn't take it and left. My Mom called and said she didn't have anywhere to go and could she come and live with me. So I went to work to support all of us and got my high school diploma at night. I was the first one in all my family to graduate from high school. Now there'll be another first. I graduate from college in June."

I want to shout. I want to embrace her and tell her she is the stuff stories are made of. But I do none of these. I only ask lamely, "How do you do it all?"

Her reply: "You just do what you have to do. So your kid's retarded. You just go on. I have good kids and soon I'll have what I've always wanted—a degree, so I can move my kids out of the ghetto."

José Wants to Be a Priest

Ten minutes into the first day of class, José Zarco enters, walks with great effort, dragging one short leg, stops in front of me and asks, "May I be in your class?" His speech is difficult and I hesitate slightly, wondering why he asks and if I am hearing him correctly. "I won't be any trouble," he adds.

I answer quickly, "Of course," and motion him to a seat where he, with great commotion, seats himself. Some watch, most turn away to study the scratchings on the chair arms. The tension is slight but clearly palpable, as if a puppeteer has pulled the strings in all our backs and then—when José, quiet and still, becomes invisible against the varicolored pattern of the class—releases them.

José waits after class until everyone is gone and then says he needs to talk to me. He shows me today's writing assignment and explains that he cannot write in class, it takes him too long; that he is handicapped because his mother had un-treated diabetes when she was pregnant. He must pass this class because he wants to graduate and become a priest.

He will type the papers, he says, on the computer in the Handicapped Center at the school. I say that will be fine, and I think we are finished but he does not go. I look away be-cause the saliva is gathering at the corners of his mouth and starting to run down his face. "Thanks for the nice class, Ms. Carol." I nod, and he shoulders his backpack painstakingly and moves awkwardly away.

Next week he brings a three-page, typewritten essay, which must have taken him hours to put on the computer. Though it has been edited by his tutor in the Learning Assistance Center, these are unmistakably his words and his feelings.

I was five years when I started to a kindergarten which was not far from my home. My mom walked me to my seat and told me to be a good boy and gave me a candy to keep me from crying. I looked around and saw many children but I noticed this particular boy named Richard who was bigger than the other kids. He seemed to be restless and all of a sudden pulled a little girl's hair in front of him so hard she started to cry. I knew he was a troublemaker and my instinct told me to stay away from him.

Five minutes later, a beautiful lady walked into the classroom. She introduced herself as Ms. Pary. I was sitting right in front of her desk. Suddenly I caught her eyes staring at me and her face lit up with a beautiful smile. She had a soft voice and gentle manner. She reminded me so much of my mother.

...As soon as the bell rang, all the children ran out for recess. Richard came up to me and started using all kinds of bad words on me. He said that I looked like a monster and walked weird. He was making fun of my disability and I was very hurt and helpless. My mother had put a handkerchief on my chest because I used to drool a lot, but Richard pulled that handkerchief from me and threw it in the swimming pool nearby. I tried to chase him but since I have difficulty in walking, I could not run fast enough to catch him. I could not help but cry out loudly, loud enough that Ms. Pary came running. I quickly clung on to her and pointed my finger at Richard. She tried to calm me down but I was so mad at Richard that I picked up a small stone and threw it at Richard. It hit him right on his forehead and he started to bleed. The principal of the school came running and immediately informed my parents. He told my parents that I should be attending a private school rather than the public school. I saw a great disappointment on my parents' faces when they heard that. But Ms. Pary spoke to the principal and said that she would keep a close eye on me if I were given a second chance. As for me, I was very determined to continue there rather than a private school or institution.

I am truly grateful to Ms. Pary for that second chance as it has taught me to become a better person and be independent, and also to accept my disability in order to go on in life. This experience taught me a meaningful lesson. I am no longer ashamed.

With José's permission, I read this essay to the class. After seconds of silence, someone begins to applaud and soon every hand is brought together in a litany of acceptance. Two girls in the front row cry but José is smiling with a grin that covers his whole face.

I Didn't Pass the SAT

Harbor College, September 1991. *Curtis Cathey ambles through the door three days into the semester and asks if he can add my class to his schedule. I consent, but ask him to see me after. I outline what he needs to do to catch up, and then he tells me he is a basketball player who made first team all-city in high school and received a scholarship to the University of Nevada at Las Vegas, but couldn't attend because he didn't pass the SAT test.*

I work full-time to support my mother and little brother so I don't have much time to study, but I need this class and I'll do the work.

He seems eager and somewhat desperate. I find myself wanting to believe he'll pass. Predictably, his first essay is full of technical errors, but so simply and authentically written I find my eyes skipping over mistakes as he writes about his family's experience with drugs:

As I was growing up, drugs were around me everyday in our black neighborhood. My brothers and cousins were dope dealers, and at the time my uncle had just died of a drug overdose. That really hit the family hard, but still, my oldest brother went on selling dope, making over eight thousand dollars a week. My other two brothers and cousins were just getting started in the drug business. I watched them go from big time to jail time and that's why I don't have nothing to do with gangs or drugs. When my brothers went to jail, my mother was crushed. I tried to be there for her because my father was sick in the hospital. My brothers got out of jail and they moved in with us. I watched how they destroyed our family by stealing, lying and even killing to get drugs. When all that was going on, my father died and my mother told my brothers that they put so

much stress on him he had a heart attack. I understand
what people mean when they talk about drugs and the
chaos it creates.

Near the end of the semester his grammar has improved
only slightly but his rhetoric and sensitivity touch me again
in an essay about his family roots:

As a young boy growing up in a small town in the United
States known as Paris, Texas, I remember my grandfather
sitting me down in his old, brown rocking chair, smoking
his pipe and talking about the heritage of our family and
the accomplishments they achieved.

I remember him telling me about one of my ancestors who
were one of thousands that passed through the under-
ground railroad to try to obtain their so-called freedom. I
can recall that well because as he spoke his eyes became
filled with tears. I guess he was trying to feel the pain my
ancestors went through in those days and times.

He also explained to me how in the 60s he and my grandmother accompanied Dr. Martin Luther King on his march
on Washington. As he spoke of the love, power and climate
of that day, I recall feeling proud of my grandparents because they were a part of history.

He also talked about how he came to Texas with nothing
except for the love of his wife and love for his country. But
with the power of the Lord and his blessings, he has been
able to have two daughters, buy a house and have three
wonderful grandchildren. He continued speaking on how
he came to Texas and on how much he loved his family. I
remember telling him, "I love you grandpa for being my
hero" and at the end of that night, I recall falling asleep in
his arms.

Halfway through the semester, I assign an essay on sports.
Of course, Curtis writes about why he likes basketball, re-

counting his experience in the process. At the end of the essay he says:

But with the power of my grandfather and the strong personality of Magic Johnson, I will continue to try to achieve my degree, and maybe play basketball at a university.

Curtis passes the class with a C.

I Have No Address

Tim Zorotovich, short, blond, with a wholesome, eager face always sits in the front row, and his hand is the first to go up when I pose a discussion question. His writing is equally open:

For one whole school year in 6th grade I didn't have an address. It was because my mother and father just got divorced. My father took off and never gave us any money. My mom couldn't find a job that paid enough so she could get a baby-sitter for my younger brother and sister.

We had a small covered trailer and that's where we lived. So when I was supposed to write my address, I just made up one because I was pretty embarrassed.

My friends always asked me why my mom picked me up hauling that trailer and I told them we were planning to go on a trip. Then I ran out of excuses and they didn't ask me anymore.

We had to use food stamps and I remember my mother would go shopping at 1:00 o'clock in the morning so no one would see her. She didn't want to be a welfare person. The whole thing was a pretty humiliating experience.

That's why I'm in school. I never want to go through that again or have my children go through that. I plan to get a good job and maybe with God's help I can make it.

Tim asks if he can be gone two weeks from school to go back into a drug rehabilitation center. "Give me extra work and I'll do all the reading." *He makes large promises but after two weeks he doesn't come back. In another week I receive an expensive, flamboyant card in the mail expressing his thanks and telling me that he is* "not doing well." *He must stay there until he's* "strong enough." *"I take two steps* forward and then one back," *he writes.* "It's hard working full-time and going to school. I just zap out sometimes. But I'll be back, don't worry."

Taipei, Taiwan, August 1970. *The drapes in the hotel room are red velvet and I draw them to see the city. From the airport we have come in an air-conditioned bus where our guide told us not to give money to the begging children because this only perpetuates the begging.*

But I am not prepared for the children jumping at the bus windows as we arrive. They could be insects, but I see they are like my own children, perhaps thinner, more ragged and dirty, with a wild desperation that strikes at me like a whip. I try to ignore them but they pull on my arms and purse until I must yank myself away and run into the hotel lobby which, magnificent and gilded, all of a sudden seems repugnant to me.

I look out of the window of my room, across the street to a muddle of dwellings made of whatever is available—cardboard, plywood, crates, canvas. Many of these dwellings are open, and, from my vantage point, I can see the floors are dirt, and only a few have mats on them. Occasionally a lone light bulb hangs from a wire as a symbol of progress. A young boy plays naked in the ditch by the side of the road which I later learn is an open sewer.

The light bulb is burned out in the table lamp, so I call and ask for a new one. A bellboy who appears to be about fifteen years old comes to the room to replace the bulb. He takes his time, seeming to want to practice his English and ask me about the United States.

"I want come United States. Very nice. Much money."

I listen.

"They have big house. Big cars." *He gesticulates.* "I go there if someone to help me." *There is a pause and he continues.* "How old I am? Say if you can. How old?"

"About seventeen," I venture with caution.

"Twenty-seven. Surprised? We look young, mostly. I have two children."

He leaves, but is back in ten minutes with another bulb.

"Here is extra for you."

"Thank you." He'll want another tip, I think.

But he begins to talk again about his dream and asks me what kind of house I live in.

"If you give me your address, I come to see you."

I write down my address and hand it to him. "Oh, California! Very nice place. Movie stars. You know any movie stars?"

Our talk is interrupted by the floor supervisor who speaks to him in Mandarin, and he leaves, probably on another errand. I find I'm vaguely disconcerted, knowing I have fed his hope in the giving of my address. I begin to unpack.

The cymbidium orchid I find on my pillow impresses me, but there is irony in the note under it: "Have a nice day."

I Am the Boy with the Oranges

Samuel Ortiz has eyes that fix intently and have such a range of response that I know he is listening, though he seldom contributes to the class discussion. He is sometimes dark and brooding, and his slight form slumps in his chair. He told me in our first interview that he is a cynic and an existentialist, that he does not believe in God, nor does he have much hope for the future of the world. Samuel makes it clear he wants an A in the class, and I outline what he must do. He comes through, and when I tell him his grade he smiles broadly and says ironically, "Vaya con Dios."

I feel shame everywhere I go. It is my shame because I am Mexican.

As I ride with some friends down the street, I see men with signs that say, work for food or I'll see boys selling oranges on the street. I see poor Chicanos with wornout clothes probably bought in La Segunda (second-hand store) or in clothes that are handed down.

My friends and I have been fortunate to have a life with not as many hardships. We have a home, food and our health; we do not have to work on streets selling food or holding signs for work. Then why do some of my friends insult and shame me by making jokes about the boy with the oranges? Why do they shame me by calling the men wih the signs beaners? Or why do they make fun of the family walking down the street with the worn-out clothes?

All of us are Mexican American, Chicanos; our origins are from Mexico and our grandfathers or fathers have had to work hard to give us this life we take for granted. Why? So we can put our cousins down or our nationality down? Why are we ashamed to associate ourselves with who we are and how we got here?

I am the boy selling the oranges on the street. I am the Chicano with the clothes bought in La Segunda. I am the man with the sign that says work for food.

But my shame isn't because of this. It is because my friends are embarrassed to admit that this is who we are. They are embarrassed by the way we look, our poverty and our culture. My friends shame me. My shame is for my friends. That is my shame.

Kim Ho Park

Kim Ho Park is a twenty-one-year-old Korean male, raised in Japan, a college graduate in biochemistry sent here to improve his English before going to graduate school. He hesitates to participate in class discussion, but his essays are fairly sophisticated and have only a few errors in English usage. In a tutorial in my office he confesses he feels terribly alone but knows that he should not. His father has left his mother for another woman and his brother is the favored son. Kim Ho came here to prove himself—and now he finds he cannot successfully communicate. I assure him that he has made himself understood to me, though I had to ask several questions for clarification. He spends days on his papers and stays after class with a list of questions to be answered. He writes:

Six years ago I was lacking in self-confidence and doubting my worth. It happened after a trivial failure, failure on an entrance examination. I knew it was a minor problem; however, it was enough to turn the sky gloomy. I struggled to find relief or salvation through literature, such as the works of Lord Byron and Anton Chekhov.

One day I happened to listen to a piano concerto of Mozart. It was brilliant, lovely music, but neither a masterpiece nor the fruit of strenuous effort. Mozart composed it just for the sake of amusing the leisured nobles on a summer night. Nevertheless, I was affected profoundly. I couldn't stand up. I shivered. As a few of the beginning notes penetrated me, I recovered some of my confidence; I felt I could manage my problems.

After that experience I have wondered what occurred to me at that moment. And now, after six years of searching the answer, I can say that we, the pianist and I, shared a certain feeling of empathy. And there was also harmony between

Mozart and me. I don't feel any hesitation to call that harmony God. I am comfortable in ascribing that astonishing
experience to encountering God.

*Kim Ho was accepted to a graduate school in the East and
moved to Florida in September. In October he called me on
the phone.* "I have a question and I have no one else to call.
First of all, I am doing fine. I record the lectures and listen
to them at home to make sure I understand everything. The
professor who is directing my research is very helpful and
has been very complimentary about my work. It is him I ask
about. He graciously invited me to his home for dinner and
to meet his wife and children. Then he invited me again but
he told me his wife would be gone. He invited me to use his
hot tub and then said if I would come, we could sleep
together. I feel hesitant about this. I don't want to offend
him because he is my teacher. Is this expected if I am to
succeed?"

*We talked about his response and his rights. I assured him
he did not have to comply and that I thought him capable of
making a decision in his own best interest.*

*I didn't hear from him for several months and then he called
to tell me he was in love with a Caucasian woman in his
class. He did not understand these strong physical feelings
and asked if I thought it was appropriate to kiss her.*

An Individual, But Not Totally

*Grant Pearse is a presence, a student of whom one is aware
as soon as he enters and whose absence cannot go unno-
ticed, not only because of his Polynesian physical bigness but
because of some openness, energy, and intelligence, almost
palpable from the first time he enters the class. He comes in
a fatigue jacket, small round glasses, three-days' dark
beard, scruffy hair—all the trappings of machismo, yet
something in his manner is gentle, vulnerable, approach-
able. As an exercise, he writes about his experience as a
Caucasian Polynesian from New Zealand coming to school in
the United States.*

Whatever the reason people come to the United States,
whether it is for escape from economic, political or social
unrest, or for adventure or just to experience another
country, we're all faced with one thing and that is that our
home culture is different from the one we experience here.

Recently I went to a farewell party for a cousin who was
leaving Los Angeles to join her family in Hawaii. And at her
party we sat on the floor, sang songs, ate, talked, played
games and did a lot of New Zealand-type things, things I am
so far away from, things that I miss. And this time helped
me to verbalize or at least organize in my mind the reasons
I am here, away from family, lifetime friends, and a culture
in so many ways similar and yet so vastly different from
this host culture.

I think of when my mother died in New Zealand and I went
back. While standing in line at the supermarket, my
mother's best friend came up to me and we embraced for
about 10 minutes, just standing there in line at the supermarket, hugging and weeping. Then this friend invited me
to her home for a special New Zealand meal, so that I
wouldn't forget that this was my home.

In the Maori tradition, the body lies in the house, just as my mother did, with a Tongan tapa cloth draped over our sturdy coffee table, and the casket on top. Then people come and visit, bring food and gifts of money. I miss the singing, the vehemence, the subtle harmonies so unrehearsed and yet so moving as to bring change into a soul. I miss the participation at the grave site, each of the family shoveling the earth onto the coffin in a final gesture of love.

Yet I love my new home here in the United States with its beauty and excitement, but am torn by its adoration of individuality and lack of community. I believe that I am an individual but not totally, as I can never separate myself from my relationship to a family, a community, the earth and God. What I do enhances these groups, and what I fail to do, fails these groups. I can't give up the Polynesian attitude that if everyone else can't rise with me, it is not worth rising at all.

Polka-Dot Family

From ponytail to clothes, Michael Haggood looks like a light Stevie Wonder. He walks into my office with a swagger perhaps born of genuine self-confidence or more likely a display of outward bravado and streetwise cockiness. As he speaks, I sense a strength, gentle and sure, an enthusiasm that infects, yet a vulnerability that seems to be the hall-mark of a confident person.

I find out Michael is about thirty years old, a teacher in downtown Los Angeles at a last-chance school for juvenile delinquents. He wants to learn how to get these kids to write and write well, in addition to improving his own writing. So we begin.

He taps in easily to core experiences and translates his feelings to paper with some fresh and particularly apt meta-phors. Mechanics are a problem and he works hard, always wanting to know why it's this way, what he did wrong, how to fix it.

Michael writes about his "Polka-Dot Family":

I have had a unique life, straddling two cultures. My father is black and my mother is a blond from Switzerland, so we have what you might call a "Polka-Dot Family." My two sisters and I are black and my brother is not only white but has blond hair....I have experienced black culture for the most part because usually what you look like is what you identify with.

In about 1966, my father had a rare day off and decided to take all of us to Ventura Beach. Mother sent us off with old plastic containers and spoons and we were so happy with the anticipation of getting out of the hot city for a day. We were on Pacific Coast Highway in Malibu when we saw a police car behind us. My dad didn't pay much attention because we weren't doing anything wrong.

Then all of a sudden there were two police cars with lights and sirens on who motioned us to the side of the highway. I remember they yelled at my father to get out and when he did, they slapped handcuffs on him, searched him, and kicked him to the ground.

We were scared and crying, not knowing what to do. The officers put him in the police car and put us in the other and drove to the police station. They put him in jail and started to quiz us. They accused my father of kidnapping white children and trying to make his get-away. My mother came down to get us, but still my father had to stay in jail three days until his name was cleared....We were scared, maybe a little bitter, but sometimes we laugh about it now....

I believe being a part of two cultures has been a great asset in my life. Though I have had challenges to overcome, I understand both sides and want to preserve what is best in each one. I am proud to be black and proud to be white but most of all I want to be a good human being.

Michael tells me about a retreat he attended on racism and intolerance with 100 high school students of all races, an event sponsored by the National Council of Christians and Jews. "At the first of the week together," *he reports,* "the kids were hostile and uncommunicative but at the end of a week of sharing experiences of racism, they were all hugging and crying and didn't want it to end. I've never seen anything like it. How can we help but love each other when we find out we have experiences in common, that we hurt, have pain and great dreams just like they do?"

3
Gangs

I see the enslaved, the overthrown, the hurt, the opprest
    of the whole earth,

I feel the measureless shame and humiliation of my
    race, it becomes all mine . . .

—Walt Whitman
"The Mystic Trumpeter"

Los Angeles, 1954. *We rent the small attic of a house near the University of Southern California owned by the widow Hernandez who does not speak English and communicates in sign language when I pay the rent or tell her the sink is stopped up or that we must do something about the cockroaches. Our rooms often smell like chilies and refried beans, and the music of the Spanish language echoes through the heating vents. For the first time in our lives we try Mexican food and love it because it is exotic, but mostly because it is cheap.*

We are the only whites on the block and if I did not have the baby, I would feel isolated. People smile at the baby when I go out with the stroller but they do not smile when I am alone. An old black man folded in an ancient upholstered chair with the stuffing coming out waves to me every day from his porch. Once I bring the baby to him and he takes him on his lap. "Mighty fine, mighty fine." This is my first friend here, and I begin to feel this neighborhood is home. I am young and naive, not afraid when my husband works nights, but he is afraid for me and keeps a loaded gun under the mattress.

I Could Smell the Blood

Lupe Martinez, one of thirteen children, Mexican immigrant, a joyous girl with an open, exceptionally beautiful face writes:

I remember the night very well, February 18, 1986 at 8:30 at the corner of Madison Street and Santa Fe. It is very clear because I was giving my boyfriend a late Valentine's card that night in our back yard. As we were talking, we heard loud screams, only we didn't think much of it since we live across the street from the park where screams are always coming from people watching games. But that night there was something different about the screams.

Then out of nowhere my nephew came running, out of breath, and told us the neighborhood gang was jumping some guy from a rival gang. As we ran towards the corner I've known so well, I felt a chill run down my spine. Step by step I got closer and then I saw the tall, dark, husky guy fall. He fell so hard on the dry grass that I could almost hear the grass being smashed by his body. I didn't see the guys running away from the scene. All I heard was the trampling of their feet. The loud noise slowly grew fainter and I was now standing in front of the body full of blood. I could smell blood and almost taste it in the air. He was beaten with a bat, stabbed in the middle of his stomach to the middle of his back. And that wasn't enough. They also shot him with a .45 revolver in the mouth so in case he lived, he wouldn't be able to mention their names.

Another thing I can't understand is how this man's friends could have just walked away from him when he needed them most. Two of his friends were in a car ready to leave. When he tried to get in, the other gang grabbed him from behind and began beating him. His friends then took the chance to get away. They turned back a few minutes later, parked across the street and watched their friend being murdered 6 to 1. They didn't have the guts to get out of their car and help him. When the police came they left as if they had done something wrong and they did; they let their friend be savagely killed.

I can't look at these homeboys in the same way anymore. Even if they are my cousins, they are animals, beasts. These are guys I grew up with, guys I have known since elementary school, guys who were always hanging around my house with my older brother. I then saw them for the kind of people they had become, brutal murderers.

River of Lagrimas

Sonia Maldonado sits on the bench in the open walkway studying as I approach her. Her dark hair is teased into a high pompadour around her pale face, and she is dressed all in black; her red lips are the only hint of color. I stop to ask her how she is doing with the extra-credit novel she is reading, The Bridge of San Luis Rey, *and we have an animated conversation about the ending and what "really" happens. Then she wants to know if she will go into Freshman English or have to take another remedial class. I have already told her she is working above the level of the class and now I let her know she is eligible, by reason of her diligence and competence, to go directly into the 101 class.*

"I was in honors English in high school. I guess I goofed on the English placement test."

"I'm sure you'll have no trouble in 101. Your writing is smooth, mechanical problems are minimal, and you seem to have a creative bent."

"People never guess I have a brain. My friends, they say I look like a gang-banger. And, you know, nobody in my family ever went to college, especially girls. My mother thinks I'm crazy. I'm supposed to find a man quick and have lots of kids. But I tell her, not now."

"What do you want to do?"

"Write. Maybe teach. Speak for Hispanic women."

Sonia tells me she has been writing poems, and she would like to put one in our publication. Here is a poem which she wrote after the death of a nephew killed by a gang member.

It is sad to see a friend has left us without
   saying good-bye.
It is sad to know a father and mother have
   lost a son.
It is sad to know they have seen their son
   selling and buying drugs in the parking lot
   of the barrio.
It is sad to know a mother has lost the son
   she carried in her womb for the happiest
   but most painful nine months of her vida,
that she took care of him when he was small
   and hungry, helped in his first steps and
   first words, that she taught him to pray to
   Diosito and La Virgen so they could be
   beside him,
that she wanted to give him the world, that
   she guided him through dark and light and
   then lost him,
that her heart is broken into tiny pieces like
   crystal when the table that supports it is
   gone.
And she will only recover her strength when
   her eyes are empty and she realizes he is
   where there is no cruelness or sadness, far
   from the hands of the cruel vida.

It is sad to know we are sad.
But it is not sad to know how happy he is in
   Diosito's warm, tender hands.
We only wish every tear we cry would bring
   him back.
But we can cry a river of lagrimas and he will
   not come.
We only drain the sorrow and the poison that
   has filled our hearts and has made it
   painful and heavy to carry.

Mommy, Where's My Daddy?

Hera is twenty-two, black, sole support of her mother and daughter and has come back to school so she can move up in her job. A colleague of mine asks if Hera is in my class and responds, "You are lucky. She is one of my favorite students." Hera is bright, open, and loving with a predilection toward being worthy of the implications of her name. She read this essay in class, gracefully tearful at the end. The class was visibly affected.

May 30, 1987 I went to visit my boyfriend to tell him I was pregnant. When I arrived he was painting his room, so I decided to put it off until later that evening. When I got home, I felt empty, my heart began to beat very fast and my mind traveled beyond unhappiness for some reason. So I decided to call my boyfriend for comfort.

I recognized his voice on the answering machine but I just hung up the phone. Then I went to his home where I found the lights on but no one was there. I sat in my car waiting for his return. A half hour went by and he didn't come. So I went home.

The next day I received a phone call. It was his sister and she said, "Bernard was killed the same day you came to visit him. Two gang members tried to take his car at the hamburger stand and they shot him in the back." I did not believe it to be true. I hung up the phone, reached for his picture, held it tight to my heart and began to cry. I thought someone would call and say it was a joke. I waited an hour and no one called so I called his mother to ask her if it was true and she said it was.

In four years of being with Bernard, every quiet moment we shared together he always asked, "When can we have a baby?" Now I was angry and hurt. How could they kill an innocent person over a car? And not only did they take one life but they scarred our lives forever. My child would never have the opportunity to know its father. But I knew I had to stay strong for my baby's sake. I knew that in spirit he would always be with us. The gang members were arrested and thrown into jail. I thought of going to see them. I wanted to let them know the pain they had caused by taking that one life.

I did go to the trial of one of the gang members to support Bernard's mother. I stared at this man who killed my baby's father. The anger was there but my thoughts were only, why? I listened closely as they repeatedly told the story. The gang member always looked around to see who was in the room. No one came to support him except his younger sister who testified of his abusive childhood. I felt sorry for her because she really loved her brother, but he let her down when he chose gangs over her. The lawyer gave her no sympathy and tortured her with questions. When she cried, the gang member showed some feelings for her and I realized this guy still had some deep feelings inside of him. This changed my heart from anger to crying out for God to help him.

After all the arguments, the jury decided he was guilty of murder. His sentence was the gas chamber. The gang member was shocked and his lawyer comforted him. As he looked over his shoulder, I looked him in the eyes.

The gang member's face is in my mind everyday. The incident travels with me daily, especially when my daughter asks, "Mommy, where is my daddy?" As I try to find the right words to tell her, my mind relives it all. My daughter is only three years old and will still ask questions until she's grown to understand what really happened.

I've been given strength through this tragedy. Learning about God has given me a more positive outlook on the situation. I have forgiven the gang member and I hope he can realize that now God is the one from whom he should ask forgiveness.

Gang-Banging

Mike Bacalso, Hispanic/Filipino writes this essay. I suggest that he might send this to the school newspaper for publication. He agrees but must remain anonymous for fear of recrimination.

I am a former gang-banger in a Filipino Blood gang and I'm going to tell you about my experience.

First, you must go through an initiation to show how tough you are. First you do "walking the line," which means you must walk in a straight line while each gang member hits you. Another one is when you stand up in one position without resisting while gang members punch, kick and even use knives on you to see how tough you are. When I had my initiation, I stood blind-folded while twenty-five gang members punched and kicked me for about five minutes. After it was over, I was barely able to walk, bleeding all over, and my rib cage was sprained. I was in pain for four days. Gang-bangers really enjoy beating the hell out of you. If you cry, they do it again. And if you think getting into a gang is difficult, getting out of it is ten times harder and more painful.

When you're in a gang, you must spend a lot of time with them and do whatever the gang leader says. These leaders enjoy taking advantage and pushing around their own members as a lesson in fear and respect. Sometimes they use their own members as scapegoats so they won't get involved in trouble. Some of these members have very low self-esteem, so they will do anything for the gang no matter what the risk. It's like their family. They tell you you will always be backed up in a fight but lots of time they cop out. They tell you that you can use your gang's reputation to scare people or to pick up girls. But mostly they steal, push people around, do graffiti, vandalize and sometimes even kill. Sometimes they get into drug dealing for the money.

One reason gangs were developed is to fight other rival gangs. There are two groups, called the Bloods and the Crips, who have a natural hatred and fight each other for territory. Sometimes this hatred is passed from generation to generation. Crips are extremely violent and enjoy killing as the ultimate excitement.

I have been in a lot of gang fights, and I am an experienced street fighter skilled in hand-to-hand combat. I always fight with my fists, but if my opponent uses a weapon on me, I will use a weapon as a means of self-defense. Personally, I enjoy fighting, but for a good cause.

I am very lucky to come out of fights with only a few bruises or cuts by stabbings because there are many people who die everyday. Now they are using automatic guns. This senseless violence is out of control, an endless struggle with no victor; everybody loses.

I was fighting once with my gang against a bunch of Crips in Compton. My friends and I were winning the fight when the gang-banger I was fighting pulled out a gun and pointed it at my head. The Crip shot at me, missing me because my friend hit him from behind. The bullet missed me by an inch, hitting a car window. After that night, I kept thinking how I almost died fighting for a stupid reason. I knew gang rivalry was stupid and not worth dying for. So I thought about getting out of the gang.

But they kicked me out and I was so severely beaten that I had to go to the hospital for injuries which took a long time to heal. I almost didn't live and still have the scars on my face. But I just couldn't see that gang-banging was any good. I knew their ideas conflicted with my morals so I placed it aside, but I can never forget.

Two years later I see a familiar face as I walk to class at CSUDH. "Mike?" He's still dressed in black. His long hair is now short and spiked. "Yeah," he says, "It's me. I graduated from Harbor. I'm here now. And you'll never guess what I'm majoring in—English. I'm doing good. I mean, doing well. Can you believe it?"

Mi Vida Loca

Rosalva Gonzalez is married, has a little boy, and works full time. Her attendance is erratic but she always has what seems to be a legitimate excuse. Most often her car breaks down.

She must finish this course, she says, so she can get a better job. I give her makeup work which she tells me later (with tears) she cannot complete. Halfway through the semester she contracts hepatitis and is unable to continue the class.

I keep her first essay:

I was an only child and always felt something was missing, like I didn't have a real family. All of that changed when I was jumped into the gang. Yes, now I was a member of the Tortilla Flats Babylocas. That was one of the happiest days of my life, so I thought.

I had gained a big family. I had my homeboys and homegirls who filled up the emptiness of not having brothers or sisters. They were going to watch over me and be there when I needed someone to talk to.

I thought I was bad. I packed my makeup on, feathered my hair, wore my big hoops and always dressed in black. I enjoyed staring down at people making them feel small, weak and afraid. I got a kick out of that superior feeling.

I basically did everything—the alcohol, the drugs and the drive-bys. I was out of control and my parents couldn't stop me. I ended up at Bay Harbor Hospital in the intensive care unit after a suicide attempt. If it weren't for my mother who found me unconscious in the bedroom, I wouldn't be here today.

I finally realized I had to change my life or else I was going to lose my life. It's a chain that never ends. Only the strong survive in a gang and the weak end up either with a drug addiction, in jail, or dead. That's why I refer to my past as "Mi Vida Loca," or "My Crazy Life."

Problem Child

Alonzo Vasquez, tall, muscular, half-Yaqui and half-Mexican, says he can't write a paper on gangs because he doesn't see any solutions.

"Why talk about it? What can you do? They are stupid. Just like I was. I was in a gang."

"Why aren't you in a gang now?"

"I got into other things. Surfing and stuff. It's just boredom. That's it. Looking for excitement or just feeling you're not good for much else."

"You have your reasons and you have your example. Now write." He left my office skeptical, but the next week handed in this paper.

I was what you would call a problem child. While I was growing up and until a year and four months ago I used and abused all types of drugs. This consistent abuse got me into a bunch of misadventures. I decided I needed an ally for self-preservation so I ran into Ricardo. He had connections with 3rd Street and Rancho San Pedro. He was a dealer and a user and we became best friends. He would supply me for free and then he gave me protection from people who would do me harm. He was the older brother figure I always wanted.

We would do everything together. I became his guardian, which I think is weird since it was me who needed protection. I started to deal drugs and contend with gangs. Ricardo's life started breaking down, so I took over and my life became a violent whirlwind. But I loved it because I was the boss.

On December 12, 1988, Ricardo was shot a number of times and beaten half to death. I blamed myself for not being there for him when he needed me. He told me to leave or I wouldn't survive. I knew he was right but I still felt bad.

It's hard to leave that life behind. It becomes the only truth you know; it's hard to change what you think you are. I quit dealing with drugs and with gangs. But Ricardo never leaves his home and snorts 100 dollars worth of drugs up his nose every day.

I discovered other thrills, like surfing and I got good at it. It's a matter of choice. Some ways seem easier than others but those shortcuts usually end in a quick death or a long and painful nonexistence....

Gangs through the Eyes of an Emergency Room Nurse

Harbor College, October 1991. *Again, as I have done for the past few semesters, I assign two essays about gangs and the class responds with papers on their own experiences. Florence Martinez, a woman about forty, is an experienced and mature writer who is taking this class as a returning student to brush up on English skills, and I appreciate the balance she lends to class discussions. The class responds to her reading of this essay with a mixture of awe and curiosity.*

Reading George Will's "West Coast Story" reminded me of the way we thought of gangs when I was younger. I agree when he wrote, "Time was when they were a rite of passage, a subculture that inner city adolescence outgrew." Who would have guessed that from a relatively small and predominantly innocent form of what could have been considered male bonding would emerge the nefarious "gangbanger," and a very real threat to our society?

In the 1950s our neighborhood gangs were largely harmless, but tough-looking, cigarette-smoking kids who hung out on street corners and the few fast-food places. If I remember correctly, they rode bicycles and sometimes even dated nice girls. Girl gangers, if any, chewed gum, wore heavy makeup and dressed wilder than average. Occasionally the gang kids carried knives or the highly unreliable zipgun which was made from a car aerial, a piece of wood, rubber bands and one .22 bullet.

In the 60s and 70s, there was much less talk of gangs. For a while it was un-cool to separate yourself from your peers; we all seemed to be flower children, equal, where everything was shared, from music to drugs to lovers. But something happened. Drugs became more and more prevalent, more sophisticated and more expensive. The sweet inno-

cence of the 60s was trampled to death by drug depen-
dence and greed. Independent dealers began making huge
sums of money. Drug users and petty opportunistic thieves
began the ripping off game. Gangs began to realize they
had the perfect infrastructure for dealing drugs. Now there
is war on our street and in our neighborhoods.

I work in an emergency room and almost every evening I
see them come in, young Hispanics or blacks—gunshot
wounds from gang fights, or drive-by shootings. Random,
thoughtless, careless shootings!

Being the mother of three sons, 14, 17, and 21, and seeing
these young boys come in scares and sickens me. I look at
them and my heart goes out to them. I imagine my own son
lying there, his heart pumping his blood through bullet
holes. But I see something else too. As soon as they know
they're not going to die, they're suddenly proud of being
shot; bullet holes make them big men. They talk of getting
even. They want nothing to do with the police or any help
in finding their assailants.

Sometimes I want to grab them and try to slap some sense
into them; I want them to realize they are playing with not
only their own life, but all of our lives. But I know it's impossible. There is no way for me to penetrate the gang
mentality, their group delusions, their subculture mores.
These are not the kids of the 50s and 60s. If there is a rite
of passage today, bullet holes and knife wounds are their
medals of honor.

Where they go when they leave, I don't know; what will
happen to them, I don't know and I'm not sure I care. I am
desensitized to their plight. Huge sums of money and
weapons of unbelievable destruction alienate me from
them; their pervasive anomie alienates me.

Sometimes in that tome of abject misery and endless hope,
I remember what the Bible says, "And this, too, shall pass."
I'm sure it will. But when? How much worse will it get
before it gets better? It seems very strange for me to look

back on the 50s gangs with a feeling of melancholy and nostalgia, but I do. I think that's a frightful commentary on our progress and our future.

Bloods and Crips: The Conflict

I ask a Samoan student, Judy Elisara, if she will get a group of her friends and relatives together to present a dance performance on Ethnic Diversity Day at Harbor College. She is not a professional, but tells me almost everyone in her culture learns to dance. She shows up with ten Samoan women in stunning costumes and they charm the audience, primarily by their own obvious enjoyment. In contrast, Judy writes of a firsthand experience with gangs.

From my personal experience I have encountered many gang-related activities. I feel that I'm caught in the middle of a war, not between two large nations or in an international dispute, but between two large groups of teenagers.

I live in Long Beach, and that's considered a Crip neighborhood. I have cousins that are in gangs and they're called Bounty Hunter Bloods. The Crips are called S.O.S. As you may already know, Bloods and Crips don't get along. Sometimes there are members with the same nationality in both of these groups, they just claim different colors.

The worst part is that the families of the gangs are always affected. My brothers are gang members, and my family is involved too, whether they like it or not. As an example, my house was shot up in a fight between two rival gang members. We called the police and told them everything but it seems like the cops were scared of being involved with a gang-related situation. We went back in the house, and my parents questioned my brothers about being in a gang. They said, "No, we're not." My sisters and I always backed up my brothers, even though we knew they were in a gang.

And the shooting didn't stop. The rival gang members stole a car and ran it into my truck. It was on a Sunday morning around three a.m. We were all sleeping in the house. I had just gotten home, got ready for bed, and I heard a great big bang. I ran upstairs to see what it was. I looked outside and it was a car that ran into my truck. I called the cops. My whole family went outside and talked to the cops. They said, "It must be gang related." I think if they did their jobs like they were supposed to, this wouldn't happen. Police cars sometimes ignore the situation when it's gang related.

It's hard to get gang members to combine together as one whole family to stop the violence. They will always have the colors of their rags in the way. It will never stop unless they decide to change on their own. That's my experience of living with gang members.

Living in the Housing Projects

Gloria Hernandez, Hispanic, about thirty-five years old with a cascade of dark, auburn hair tells her story.

Living in the projects is no place for raising children. These projects are on the west side of town, also known as "Wilmas" for Wilmington.

The projects have their own police that patrol the area constantly. Here in the projects you have two gangs, one called the Bloods and then you have the West Side Wilmas gang. From the looks of it, the gangs don't really fear the police.

I lived in the projects for four months with my sister. That was all I could take. I knew of drugs and gangs but I didn't know how bold these people are. Loud music played every night to early morning. Gunshots sounded nightly. I would pray every night that one wouldn't come through the window anywhere near where my kids were sleeping.

Everyday and night there are drive-by shootings. The worst of it all is that there are a lot of kids playing outside who see all this and are targets for flying bullets. But no one cares, and everyone is afraid of saying anything because of gang retaliation. The saddest thing is you can already see the little kids getting pulled into what they see, drugs, money and guns. Six-year-olds run around calling friends, "Hey Blood" and the mothers think it's cute. They even see people using crack because these people don't hide anything they do.

Practically everyone there is selling drugs. They stand right in front of your house and sell. They stop cars, waving people down, doing whatever they have to to make a sale— little kids, big kids, and even old men and women are selling. There is no age limit in this game.

Then the drug dealers talk to the kids, showing off their
money and giving the kids a few dollars so the kids yell out
"One time," meaning "The police are coming." These kids
see the bundles of money, rings and gold chains on these
guys, so they end up thinking that's the way to make
money. There is no hope in this area for the young. Even if
they don't want to join a gang, they will probably be forced
to join one, one way or another.

*Gloria moved out of the projects into her boyfriend's home,
but last week came running to my car as I drove into the
school parking lot. Her hair was disheveled and house slip-
pers flapped on her feet. She couldn't bring in her final
papers, she said, because her boyfriend had told her to get
out of the house and changed the locks so she couldn't get
in. Since she spent so much time at school, he accused her of
having an affair and told her he thought school was "a
bunch of nonsense." She is faced again with having to move
back to the projects. Her mascara is running.* "I'm sorry to
cry," *she says,* "I just have nobody to talk to."

Dino

November 1992. *Dino Bermudez sits in class with large purple-black bruises showing at the sides of his sunglasses, the first time he has been to class this week. An A student, he has never missed before. After class he walks to my desk, limping slightly.* "Sorry I missed. I had a little trouble—"

Another student interrupts with a question. I take her paper and her explanation but I am thinking about Dino. In the first-of-the-semester interview he told me of a difficult family situation that he said might affect the quality of his school-work. His father was physically and mentally abusive, so he had moved out. He had to work full time and had little time to study.

"My parents don't really want me around," *he had said.* "Nobody really cares. Except one teacher in high school. She said I could pretty much be whatever I wanted to be." *These thoughts replay quickly, and when the other students are gone, I ask, "Dino, was it your father?"*

"Oh no. I just had some trouble."

I raised my brows and looked with a question.

"A fight. I was in a fight."

"Gangs?"

"No. I told you—that's behind me. But those guys could have been gang members. I don't know. Probably."

"What happened?"

"Well, I went to my niece's baptism at church. My sister wanted to go home right after, so I walked out of the

64

church with her to my car. I was all dressed up, tie and everything. These black guys came out of nowhere and started calling me names, like the names they have for Mexicans. I yelled back. They lit on me and beat me up. My sister screamed but nobody was around. They beat me unconscious. I think they were drunk. Just looking for trouble."

"Where was this?"

"In front of the Catholic church. In Compton."

"Are you going to be O.K.?"

"Oh yes. I just need to keep my mouth shut. Can you give me the assignments I need to make up?"

I give him the assignments and he leaves with the comment, "No, it wasn't my father this time. Don't worry. This kind of stuff happens all the time."

4
L.A. on Fire

Man cannot live as nothing but an object, as dice thrown out of a cup; he suffers severely when he is reduced to the level of a feeding or propagating machine....Man seeks for drama and excitement; when he cannot get satisfaction on a higher level, he creates for himself the drama of destruction.

—Erich Fromm
The Anatomy of Destructiveness

Flashes of Defiance

Sunday, May 3, 1992. *The ashes still smolder from the weekend rioting in south central Los Angeles as we drive to a shelter to deliver food and clothing. The presence of the National Guard, the marines from Camp Pendleton, and the LAPD around the gutted-out city blocks make me feel I am in Beirut, or perhaps a Third-World country—not the United States.*

As we unload the food and clothing, we notice a Hispanic family coming toward the loading dock—a husband, wife, small child, and a baby. They ask if we have any food and are told by the man in charge to come back in an hour when the sorting is finished. I do not know their circumstances, but I do know the local grocery stores have been looted and destroyed. The family continues walking down the littered street, pushing the baby in a stroller.

Tuesday, May 5, 1992. Harbor College. *The riots are first in everyone's mind, precluding any discussion of assigned material. I ask the students to write about what they felt that Thursday afternoon and evening. Alicia, one of the black girls and an A student writes:*

When I got home my feelings were hurt, but not just hurt. I felt angry and sad. I was angry because it took all the rioting, looting and Rodney King getting beat before people could see that there is a problem. I felt sad for my black people because they get harassed and pushed around and finally I thought they were going to get some justice. Then I sat and listened to 12 people tell my people their lives meant nothing. Nobody listens when we try to tell them what's going on. It took violence to get something done. I felt like burning something down too. I feel sorry for people who were hurt, but that's what it took. I wasn't on the streets looting and burning because I had somebody to talk me out of it. I have a feeling inside me I don't know how to explain. I don't want to be prejudiced, but I just don't know.

Samoan student "Lou" Liulu relates:

On Thursday I couldn't attend school because of all the looting happening by my house. I had to stay home because I am the only male at the house. It was my duty to protect the most important thing in my life: my mom. She was so shaken up because everything was happening right in front of my house. I was scared, but I wouldn't let my mother know. We were prisoners in our own home.

Cheryl Hunter raises her hand and asks to read her essay which is excerpted here:

It really hit me on Friday when the riots and fires were going on. My friend and I went into a grocery store in Long Beach and all the white people stared at us suspiciously, like they wondered what we were thinking. When I got back to the car, I began to cry when I realized that because of the color of my skin, I would never be accepted, especially since the riots. If I hadn't been raised the way I was I would be out there looting because I just did not care anymore. The anger I felt was indescribable. Most people don't even understand why the riots took place. They don't know what it's like to be black. They can never know what we've been through.

Richard Engleman, white, and a nurse at County-USC Medical Center, asks if he can state his perspective:

Thursday evening I walked into the hospital and it was a war zone. Every few seconds you could hear shots fired outside. Injured people were afraid to go to the hospital. The supplies, which are usually very scarce, were totally depleted. The entire hospital was in total confusion because many nurses could not get to work. Only critically injured people were cared for. People with lacerations were given dressings to put on themselves. No sutures were performed due to lack of supplies and manpower. There was a needless loss of life. I personally felt anger and disbelief at how people could act like animals.

Cheryl is crying now. She turns to where Richard had taken his seat and says vehemently, "You just don't know."

Richard raises his voice. "Violence is not the answer. The blacks are just cutting off their own arms!"

The tension is palpable. Several others enter the discussion with primarily emotional responses—responses that reflect the frustration, the paradox, the complexity of this dilemma. We run over the class time, and I attempt to achieve some sense of closure. I remember a statement from a long-ago Shakespeare class, an idea I have occasionally tested against experience. I sense its appropriateness now: "The greatest conflicts of the world are not right against wrong, but right against right."

May 15, 1992. *Nothing has changed in my neighborhood since the Los Angeles riots. Children laugh and play in the swimming pool next door, the birds sing in the eucalyptus trees, and girls with long blond hair ride horses up the bridle path at the side of my house. The riots on television were frightening and some people may have been temporarily inconvenienced, but the dominant emotion was gratitude that it all happened twenty miles away.*

It is precisely this distance that has always been the problem—the prevailing idea of "them" and "us." The ability to retreat to a haven, to blame others, and to be unaware it will happen again is to say that our togetherness has become irretrievable.

Every Black Man Is a Potential Rodney King

Across my desk sits Melvin Stokes, a forty-year-old black custodian for the Compton Unified School District who, at the strong suggestion of his school principal, has come back to the university to get his degree. We have worked on a number of papers he's doing in other classes; his writing seems clearheaded and to the point.

"You're not going to believe this," *he says, fumbling with some papers from his backpack. He produces a paper he's completed for another class and points silently to a large A marked on the cover sheet.* "I've showed this to everybody. My principal, the teachers, my relatives. I'm proud. I can do it."

"You are doing it." We talk for a while and then go on to a new subject for his next paper—the L.A. riots. "How do you feel about the riots?" I ask.

"I wasn't surprised it happened because of all the anger I hear from other blacks, from the anger I felt and feel."

"Anger about what in particular?"

"Lack of jobs for blacks, lack of opportunity, just an overall frustration with the system."

"System?"

"Yes, the government and the way it allows police to beat or even kill the innocent. The Rodney King incident was just a magnified example of something that happens all the time, and I mean, *all* the time. A young black male in Los Angeles is always subject to being a Rodney King."

"Has this happened to you?"

"I've been pulled over so many times you wouldn't believe it—for nothing—just because I'm big and black. When I was about thirty years old, a couple of white policemen pulled me over at about 118th and Main and made me get out of the car and put my hands on the hood of the car. They took my wallet and began to look through it and saw pictures of some of my female friends. One of them said, 'Hey, partner, look at this fine bitch. Does she have a sister?' I couldn't take it, so I said, 'How would you like me to look in your wallet to see if you have any fine white bitches I can look at?' He slammed my head down on the car with his left hand and pointed his revolver at me with his right hand and said, 'I did kind of like you. But now I should blow your damn head off.' Then he yelled to his partner, 'Run a check on this guy.' They found I had a couple of unpaid traffic tickets, so I was arrested and jailed for two days. This is not uncommon, believe me. We all thought when the Rodney King video came out that people would finally see what's happening with black males and the police. When that verdict came down that those cops were not guilty— pow! I just knew something was bound to happen."

"How did you feel when you heard the verdict?"

"Mad as hell. But I didn't do the rioting and looting. Violence is just not the way. I will tell you, though, I was right there in the 60s during the Watts riots."

"Did you live in Watts?"

"No, I lived in Compton, but all my roots were in Watts. And my anger was inbred—my dad and uncle always talked about rough treatment by the police. My dad believed my uncle was killed by the police because my uncle was a hard drinker and liked white women. He was found shot in the head up near Bakersfield and we never did find out who did it. So I was prepared for the Watts riots. I was only fourteen years old then and my friend's father loaded a bunch of us in the back of a truck and we went down and looted, right where all the action was. Man, that was a supreme feeling of euphoria! I came home and shared the loot—cigarettes, liquor and candy—with neighbors. We felt powerful at last."

"What do you think will fix it?"

"It's not about disagreement between Koreans and blacks, or Hispanics and blacks. It's about jobs, fair and equal opportunity, and the need for change in the structure of the police department. Crime comes out of not having fair and equal opportunity."

"Do you feel you can be anything you want to be?"

"That's what I'm trying to do. But it's hard. I went to Sears to buy shirts and couldn't get credit. I have a good job, money in the bank, other credit cards, but I couldn't get credit. Things like that happen all the time. And some people aren't as lucky as I am to get a job. Those jobs just aren't out there or some poor people may not have a car needed for a job. They can't go to school because they have no money. My mom and dad had ten kids and we're all doing o.k., but most of the time I'm made to feel second-class. But I'm not into violence. I just want to work in the system, go to school and better myself."

"Do you think the riots are over?"

"No, because the problem isn't over. The riots didn't solve anything."

It Was a Nightmare

Latisha Fahie, another black student, responds:

My sister and I were on our way back to her apartment at Loyola when we heard on the radio that the verdict was in and the four officers who were accused of beating Rodney King were not guilty. I just froze with my mouth wide open. My sister and I were in shock. We couldn't believe what had happened.

The first thing that came to my mind was to hurt someone. The second thing was the question, "Why doesn't the justice system work for black people?" It just isn't fair.

When we reached the apartment, we turned on the TV and couldn't believe what we saw. I felt like it was something out of a bad nightmare.

And did it improve race relations? In a way it did and in a way it didn't. I think now people realize there is a lot of hatred and pain that black people feel. This has been going on for hundreds of years and now it's coming out. It came out in the Watts riots and now in this one. History just keeps repeating itself and we need to say "Stop!" We're destroying ourselves. We need to come together as one and live in peace. At least people came together after the riots and gave food and clothes. But I'm sorry, that's just not enough.

Violence Defeats Itself

Myra is black and sits stoically in the back of the class, murmuring asides to those next to her, never moving her head or changing her expression. "I hope we discuss some real issues in this class," *she says to me after class early in the semester.*

"Like what?"

"Like abortion. Like the L.A. riots." *I assure her we will.*

That next week we discuss an excerpt in our text from Martin Luther King's Stride toward Freedom *in which he discusses three ways oppressed people deal with their oppression. King says that some oppressed people simply give up, as characterized by the words of an old song, "Been down so long that down don't bother me."*

Other oppressed people resort to violence and hatred, but this brings only momentary results, according to King. We read aloud: "It [violence] solves no social problem; it merely creates new and more complicated ones....Violence is immoral because it thrives on hatred rather than love. Violence ends by defeating itself" (as quoted in Warner, Hilliard and Piro 1992, 212). The students are inordinately quiet.

The third way suggested by King is the way of nonviolent resistance. "With nonviolent resistance, no individual or group need submit to any wrong, nor need anyone resort to violence in order to right a wrong" (213). I ask for a response and the ensuing discussion is heated. I hear the following comments:

"Sometimes you gotta be violent. People don't listen any other way."

"But what did it help? Look what happened."

"I'm not justifying violence. I'm just saying that now maybe people will listen."

"The police are violent. Are we supposed to just sit by and take it?"

I ask them to consider what King is saying and then write about their experiences and feelings during the riots. This is Myra's personal response after our discussion.

April 29, 1992 was a day I will never forget. I had just come home from school around three o'clock and my neighbor told me riots had begun in downtown Los Angeles. I ran in the house to call a friend who lives there and the phone rang over and over. No calls were getting through.

I went straight to my mother's house and when she was not there, I was uneasy. Then she walked up behind me and I threw my arms around her. "Mother, what's going on?" She told me to calm down and go in the house. We turned on the television and I was overwhelmed by the destruction that was going on before my eyes. My feelings were hurt as I watched. All the landmarks in my former neighborhood were burning down. The first store I had ever walked to by myself when I was a little girl was just a pile of ashes. That day, April 29, seemed to last forever. I watched television for twenty-four hours straight, numb from head to toe. My feelings were mixed; I was afraid and angry at the same time.

The second day of the riot, I felt so ashamed of the people who participated in the destruction. Then I was also ashamed of the people who caused it. That day, I realized there's not much difference between people and animals. I agree with Dr. King—that violence defeats itself.

I Wanted to Go Back to the Philippines

May 1991. *Elisa Baby Castro from Manila has been in Los Angeles about five years. She sits in the front row, wide-eyed, diminutive, quiet, almost fitting her middle name. She writes about her feelings the first afternoon and evening of the riots.*

I felt so sad and upset Thursday because the Payless Shoe store where I work was broken into and shoes were stolen. But we were glad it wasn't burned. When I came to school, I heard a lot of noise about what was going on and I felt so worried and scared about the results of things. When I got to class, they were still talking and arguing about justice or injustice. It is so difficult to know who is really true.

I turned on the TV the first thing when I got home to get an update. I kept mentioning God and praying. Then in the afternoon I went to work and saw the store door was broken down. I felt upset and so scared because I saw a lot of people crowding in the grocery store and the bank. I felt there was a war going on and I felt like I wanted to go back to the Philippines. We closed the store because everywhere around was looted and burned.

It Gave Me a Heavy Heart

Cecelia is an Asian medical lab technician married to a man of Dutch descent. Early in the semester she writes about being accosted by security in the Carson mall as she shopped with her blond baby. The baby was crying and the police said, "If the baby were yours, you could keep it quiet. Did you kidnap this child?" They detained her in the mall until she produced her identification. They checked her car and made several phone calls before they released her. She was humiliated.

Now she writes about her feelings during the L.A. riots:

At 7:00 o'clock, during my lunch break at work in Los Angeles, I heard that disruptions had spread with more looting and hundreds of fires throughout the Los Angeles area. I became very disturbed. People at work were saying blacks were shooting whites, and whites were shooting blacks and that Koreans were also targeted. The news scared me because my husband is white and I am Asian. I was afraid because I realized that the primary reason for the uprising was about color and race.

When I arrived home that night, I watched the television news coverage and it gave me a heavy heart. My children did not go to school the following day and I could not go to work for several days. There was an ugliness about the whole thing. The usual afternoon smog was replaced by a thick layer of black smoke.

But nevertheless, I was with Edward James Olmos' group of volunteers who started clean-up of the riots with brooms and shovels. I felt obligated to help after the unrest, only because I prefer to erase in my mind the ugliness of the riots. To me, there was nothing good about it. It brought more problems and miseries: Deaths—52; Injuries—2,383; Cost—$735.1 million; Jobs lost—up to 20,000; Buildings damaged—4,000 plus; Businesses destroyed—6,000 plus.

Rodney King, having become a symbol of the unrest, quite simply asked, "Can we all get along?" This big question always pops into my mind with negative answers.

Yashunda

Yashunda Jones, a young, single black mother of three ("and one is white," she says) is conferring with me about her essay—a narrative about the riots in which several details are omitted that would make the story more cogent. The writing is vehement with exclamation points, words in large capital letters—like spots of unmitigated passion. I ask her to tell me more about the story.

"Well, I just wanted to say I didn't go out and riot, but I had friends and relatives who did. But I felt like doing it. I stayed home because I don't believe in breaking the law. But I was glad to see something finally happen. I'm just saying all this was necessary to get people's attention."

"What people?"

"All those people who don't treat us like human beings. Like I work as a nurse's aide in an emergency room. A white woman came in last week with her sick daughter and wanted me to take her in that minute. A lot of people had been waiting a long time and I told her we'd get to her as soon as possible. She screamed at me and said, 'Get out of my way, you black bitch.' I went for her, but my coworker held me back or she'd have been flat on that floor. It's just lots of things like that. Like when I go shopping, the clerks follow me around real suspicious, like I'm going to steal something. It's that way when you're real black like me. Don't get me wrong. My sister married a white guy and I get along with him. My kid is half-white—what do I tell him? I say love the people that love you and forget the rest."

Yashunda sighed, paused only briefly and continued. "You know it's not over."

"You mean the prejudice?"

"Well, that. But I mean the riots. I have a couple of nephews in gangs and they say they're just waiting. They have guns they picked up in the looting and they say right out, 'We're just waiting. This time, we're going to win.'"

"What do you think could prevent another riot?"

"Nothing. They're a little crazy and desperate."

"Desperate for...?"

"To be something, I guess. I know that's not the way to do it but I wonder what will."

"You're doing it."

"What?"

"Getting an education. Getting off welfare and building your self-esteem."

"Esteem? I always had esteem. It's all those people that can't look past a black skin and see that you have guts and feelings. It's feeling like you don't have power, like nothing you do can take you out of your skin."

Stop the Madness

September 1992. *The campus climate is nearly normal but vestiges of the May unrest surface in bathroom graffiti and an occasional slight ruffling of feathers in class exchanges. Open forums have been held for anyone in the campus community who felt a need to speak. Dr. William Blischke of the sociology department, researching campus climate and cultural diversity, reports in the Alumni Paper, Fall 1992, that "a majority feel that their ethnic group is well integrated with other ethnic groups on campus, and many feel that we, as a university, have played a positive role in increasing their sensitivity."*

Joseph Moss, Associate Director of the Physical Plant at CSUDH reports in an article by Pamela Hammond, "Out of the Ashes," also in the Alumni Paper, that his life has been irrevocably changed since the Los Angeles riots. "It was the most devastating thing I've encountered in my life," *says Moss, a forty-six-year-old African American and leader in the Bethel African Methodist Episcopal Church in Los Angeles. In April, he and the men's group of the church discussed the continuing erosion of the black family and planned a rally with the theme, "Stop the Madness." They also met prior to the Rodney King trial to prepare for whatever decision was made in the case. Plans were made and announced over the air to gather at the First AME Church. Moss says that when the decision came down his* "mouth went dry and a fear came over me that was just unbelievable." *Moss left work and went down to the church to help. Volunteers poured into the church, offering food and services— a white, male plumber, several members of the Korean community, and many others. The church invited gang members to come to the church and they came. Moss says:*

"Again I found myself in a situation that I thought I'd never be part of, talking to these young men, listening to their side of what's going on. They have hopes and dreams, too.

"Many want to stop. Not all, but some of them want out. They don't have a door. We've offered them a door, a home or place for those who just want to sit and talk.

"I was part of a gang in San Francisco when I was growing up. The inner cities have always had gangs. That was part of the survival. So I understand part of what they're talking about.

"Those who tell me that people don't want to work together, well, that's a myth. As a people, we do care."

5
A Richer Stew

Many spices make the stew richer.

—Mahatma Gandhi

Rolling Hills, September 1973. *My husband receives a late telephone call informing him that the fourteen-year-old son of a Samoan patient of his has been killed—shot by an unknown gunman as he came home from church in the back of a pickup truck. When we ask if we can be of any assistance, George Malemaleuna, the twenty-year-old brother, invites us to his home, with the explanation that* "this is part of our culture, to gather together at the home." *He adds,* "If you feel comfortable."

We travel a half-hour to a housing project, Hawaiian Gardens, and after some difficulty, find the apartment in which the Malemaleunas live. We are welcomed by George into a small living room with no furniture, only a straw mat covering the floor on which Samoan family and friends are seated against the wall. All the women and some of the men wear lava-lavas, a drape of printed material wrapped around and fastened at the waist. We are introduced and acknowledged with a nod or two, then motioned to a place on the floor with George beside us.

The conversation is in muffled Samoan and not directed at us, but the Polynesian openness and acceptance is palpable though we are strangers in this relatively private ritual. Their faces are neither sad nor happy, but stoic, except as I look at one of the women who acknowledges my gaze with a broad smile and nod. I learn from George that she is the mother.

George, who seems to be the only one who speaks English, explains they are saying this is the first time whites have visited their home and they are happy to have us. We are served a fruit drink by one of the older women and notice that no one else has one.

George says the family and friends get together like this for sometimes three days to comfort one another and have a good time. "And we all dress in white for the funeral. This is our way."

My husband speaks to the father as he leaves, hoping some of his words are understood, or if not, that the warmth of his handshake and empathy and support are felt.

Earthquakes and Other Challenges

Arturo Camarillo is short, about twenty-eight years old and were it not for his eager innocence, would appear to be a proto-typically dashing, mustached Latino. Arturo has been in the United States just two years from a small town in the interior of Mexico, about a four hours' bus ride from Oaxaca. He sits in the front row, face upturned, always present and participating.

One day, he doesn't come to class. The next week, he returns with an apology. "I am very sorry, but something terrible happened. I was hit by a drunk driver. He hit me on the passenger side at 45 mph, and my little old car did two rolls. I was upside down when it stopped. All the people who pulled me out said I should give thanks to God. It is incredible that I am alive. But now I have no car, so I could not come to school. But my friend, he said I could use his old bike, so now that is how I get around. It is many miles to school, but I will be here from now on. This is just another challenge I have."

I find out what he means when he responds in an essay to a quote about approaches to difficulties in life.

Since I was a child I had in mind to graduate from a university; however, when you don't have money, there is not a chance. It doesn't matter how clever you are. My family is very poor, nevertheless, my parents sent me to the university in Mexico City with much hardship. I studied there with very little money. I ate just once a day. I suffered a bit; however, I felt happy everytime I got good grades. Then came the big earthquake. I was saved because I was at school, but my house and all my belongings in the world were buried in the rubble. I didn't know what to do.

My brother said I could come to Los Angeles and live with him and get a good job. But now in the United States, I am still having a difficult time. When I came, my brother got me a job as bus boy at Marie Callender's. I felt like I was on another planet. The boss asked me to fill the water glasses and I didn't understand English. I began to clear the table. The other waiters and the customers began to laugh. I went into the bathroom and cried a little because I felt like a worm. I decided to desert immediately. When I got home, I carefully analyzed the problem. My problem was English. I would go back to school and learn to speak. That's why I am here. I want to excel and someday I will own my own restaurant in this beautiful country.

Just last week Arturo told me his check from financial aid had been lost and that he wouldn't receive a replacement for six weeks. He was now living on his own and had no money.

"I did not want to tell my mother back home my predicament but my brother told her. And you know what? My mother sent me a letter and in it was money for a trip home for Christmas. I don't know where she got the money. I think maybe all the neighbors got together and collected money. Christmas is so wonderful in my little village. We make clay figures to remind us of the Holy Family and then we have a birthday party for Diosito. We have a midnight procession to his manger and sing lovely songs to adore him. Then we give hugs to each other—it is the key to keep my little village united. Life is good when you have love and something to believe in. Somehow things work out for me."

As I drive home that last day of the semester I remember our trip to Mexico City at Easter when I watched as a woman walked on her knees over the cobblestones leading to one of the most sacred shrines of Catholicism. I didn't know how long she had been crawling, but her knees were bleeding and a child walked beside her crying for her to stop. I was so affected that I turned away with tears both for her pain and for the depth of her devotion and belief. Though this kind of self-punishment is not a part of my philosophy, I marveled at the faith. And I feel quite sure today that Arturo Camarillo will eventually have his own restaurant.

Miyako Wants Another Husband

Miyako Yamaguchi, wife of a wealthy Japanese executive, is diminutive, soft-spoken, has been in the United States eighteen months, wears pricey, fashionable clothes and has work-of-art handwriting. She confesses:

I'm actually wife and a mother. But one of my friends recently divorced because her husband was an unreliable man. She said she would make several conditions when she married next time. If I were her, what would I want in a husband?

I want my husband to change useless electric bulbs for new ones and drive nails on the wall for paintings. I want my husband to plan the menus, cook and do the dishes on weekends and not be volatile, periodically. I want my husband to clean the rooms on weekends. I want my husband not to use credit cards too much without checking the bank account. I want my husband to exercise to keep in good shape. I want my husband to hang his suits in the closet when he comes home. I want my husband not to go to bed before I finish clearing the dinner table. I want my husband to get up early without procrastination in the bed. I want my husband to put the bed in order. I want my husband to take three weeks vacation to travel abroad with the family in summer. I want my husband to pay the expenses from his own savings, not from the household expenses. I want my husband to not address me when I'm reading a book. If I find another person more suitable as a husband, I want the liberty to divorce him with California laws.

I Wasn't There

Keiko Shimada, wife of a Japanese diplomat and mother of two small children, reports she was not aware of her "Japaneseness" until she came to the United States. "In Japan, everyone is the same, but here I am a minority and much more conscious I am Japanese." *She writes the following in a class exercise after a discussion about nuclear war:*

As I am a Japanese, I have been brought up listening to Hiroshima and Nagasaki stories like nursery rhymes. I'm almost at the point of being fed up with these stories. Especially am I in August when we have to watch documentaries on TV connected to Hiroshima day. We are repeatedly told the same kind of stories by the people who actually experienced Hiroshima and lost many of their dear people because of the atom bomb. Those people are already in their fifties and sixties and they are disappearing. We have a new generation that does not know about this from experience.

Yes, we need these people as story-tellers even if we Japanese are fed up with those stories. The earth needs the story of these people to save herself.

Close to Death

Tiffany Muller, class energizer, is bright, outspoken, Jewish, raised by a single mother and, at eighteen, lives in her own apartment. She has supported herself since she was sixteen by teaching aerobics. She also goes to school full time and is the paradigm of success and competence. She surprised us all with this essay and unashamedly reads it to the class.

I had an experience that almost ended my life. This experience was with drugs. Two years ago, I was heavily into cocaine. I'm sober now, but I'll always be an addict.

It all started when a few of my friends were buying quarters of coke. When they did a line, it seemed as if they were the happiest group of people and I wanted to feel that happiness.

My friend Laura and I went to a dealer's house and purchased a half, which is two quarters of cocaine. I did a line and my nose burned, but the feeling from the coke took away the burning sensation. It was by far the greatest feeling I've ever felt. For the next month, I did cocaine every day. I started out by buying quarters, then halves, then G's and so on. I was spending money like crazy.

My friends told me I was getting carried away, and I was becoming an addict. At the time, I didn't believe them and since they kept bothering me about the cocaine, I did my drugs alone.

As my addiction grew and I ran out of money, I found another way to get cocaine. I stole it from my dealer's house. One night I went there to buy an eight ball because I just received my check from work. At that time, I was coming down from my high. When I knocked on the door, no one was home. I went around to the back window to see if they were asleep and noticed the window was open. I pulled off the screen and climbed into the window. I knew where they kept the cocaine, so I stole it and ran out of the house as fast as possible without stopping to look back. I got in my car and drove home. I was so nervous. When I got home, I looked to see how much I had stolen. I had stolen a half ounce, which was approximately nine hundred dollars worth. I thought I would never have to buy cocaine again.

Within the next week, I did the entire half-ounce. I overdosed on cocaine; I just couldn't stop. I no longer felt the happiness. I felt pain. I couldn't breathe, and my heart skipped beats. Worst of all, I had severe chest pains. I hadn't slept or eaten for over a week. By then, I weighed only seventy-six pounds.

I thought if I were to go to sleep the pain would cease to exist. I was wrong. In that moment I was near to death. Next thing I knew, I was lying in a hospital bed. I could have saved a lot of time and money if I had shot myself. It's the same thing.

It's been over two years since I've done cocaine and it will be an eternity until I ever do it again. Take my word for it. Never do drugs.

Nada

Los Angeles Harbor College, September 1991. *Dressed entirely in black, Keith Faulkner makes his usual three-minutes-late appearance in class, wearing a tuxedo coat with satin lapels and tails, a black derby hat and very pointed suede boots—complete with long hair, dyed jet black.*

The class titters. I cannot ignore so auspicious an entrance, so I thank him for making our class "not boring." He makes a screwy face, folds his tall frame into the chair and places his white, long-fingernailed hands ceremoniously over his notebook.

His first paper describes how he has been shamed all his life for being stupid, that he has been told his brain just shorts out sometimes. His paper is impassioned yet cogent, if not superior in its logic and sophistication. Yet most words are spelled phonetically and I recognize he is probably dyslexic.

I read his paper anonymously to the class and they respond with comments like, "He or she doesn't write dumb. Why would teachers say that to this person?"

In our first interview, we talk about his background, and I find he quit high school, "because I was bored out of my gourd," *and because* "I didn't like being told I was stupid." *He told me he stayed home, wrote poetry and novels, composed music on his synthesizer, and read Dostoevski, Nietzsche and Sartre.* "Sartre is my favorite. Camus, too. They're all so dark and that's the way life is. Life has no meaning you know. Absolutely none."

I ask him what makes him want to live, then, and if he has moments when he is happy.

"Only when I'm reading, when I block out the world. I feel so absolutely different from everyone else in every way that I am only happy when I do this. And I keep on living because I must write. I feel I must leave something, some product that keeps on after I die."

We talk at length. I mention dyslexia and he says he has never been diagnosed officially, but that someone mentioned it once. I ask him to see dyslexia as a physical handicap, a difficulty in seeing rather than a defect of personality or mentality. He will be given the same allowance given to others with physical challenges when he takes the writing exam to exit college.

I think Keith knows he is bright. But he knows that intellectual awareness and artistic sensibility, along with dyslexia, separate him from others. And though he lives with his parents who love him, he feels totally unlike them. Girls are too much trouble and boys are too competitive. "Being and nothingness is my creed," *he proclaims.*

He shows me his novel which replicates the nada *tone of Hemingway. Yet for all this nothingness, he strives to do well, turns in all papers typed and on time, and begins to share his work freely with the class. And still he arrives late in black tails, giving witness again and again to his reaching.*

Nigerian Black Magic

Patrick Iberosi, who is from an Ibo village in Nigeria, comes in for his first tutorial and sees a copy of Things Fall Apart *by Chinua Achebe on my desk. Quite coincidentally, this novel documents life in a Nigerian Ibo village before white contact, and he is so excited he can hardly get the words out.*

"You read that? I can't believe it. I have part of that book memorized. That is our story."

We talk at length about his background and he tells me he was educated in an elementary school near his village (Achara Umuaka), went to a Catholic high school, and then came to the United States to go to college. He is now a graduate student working on his master's thesis and needs to improve his English diction. He hands me the following practice essay in preparation for the Graduate Writing Exam which he must take in order to continue his graduate studies in business:

Juju is a part of my culture which I liked as a little boy without understanding its implications. Juju means poison and witchcraft. To practice Juju, you go to a powerful native doctor specializing in traditional medicine and witchcraft who will invoke a spirit against a person, family or group. It is done with various objects such as a baby toy buried in your compound, or a powder spread in your meal, or money as a gift.

The object of Juju is to kill one's enemy by means of a silent process. The native doctor is approached with money, kola nut and goat. Rituals are performed and the Juju acts on the victim. The signs of Juju include: severe headache, loss of appetite, constant talking and acting up, cough, fever and heart attack.

If a spirit is invoked against someone it usually results in the death of the victim, though death is not feared as much as the agonies and miseries one goes through to reach the end. The spread powder in meal acts as a catalyst to speed up the reaction in the body. If a baby toy is buried in your compound it will menace your family forever unless dug out and removed. The gift of money will paralyze you forever. Juju can also make you cough "as long as the cord of life shall lengthen." The only protection is to consult another powerful Juju man and give him a huge amount of money. But even then, it may not work.

As a little boy, I enjoyed telling my enemies that I would put Juju on them. I did not fully understand the implications of my statement. I was childish and I did not mean any harm. I grew up to understand and hate Juju. Now the question is always in my mind, "Will someone put Juju on me?"

If the Ibo community is to survive, education, civilization and integration into modern freedom are necessary. The Juju man is primitive and sees witchcraft as a means of monetary success and power. But with Juju we are not free. With education all the evils of witchcraft will be dropped. Juju is an evil against both the individual and society and should be abolished.

In the process of the semester Patrick's story unfolds. He worked hard to pull himself out of the poverty he was born into by getting an education and subsequently investing in a highly successful business and working for the government. He came to the United States to further his education and "to improve his status."

Alone and lonely in an apartment house in Los Angeles, he was vulnerable to the attentions of a girl in the same complex who told him she could no longer pay for her apartment and asked if she could move into his temporarily, "maybe for a week." She was kind, solicitous and grateful, and he saw no harm in telling her about his financial success as they moved in to an intimate relationship. And being a good Christian, he felt they should marry, which they did.

Then he found she did not come home at night and was sometimes gone with her friends for days at a time. And Patrick, having heard about the freedom American women have, thought perhaps he should be tolerant of this behavior. Then he began to notice money missing from his wallet, which he initially blamed on his own absent-mindness. Then large amounts began to disappear, and he confronted her, thinking perhaps she had borrowed it and forgotten to tell him about it. She said yes, she had taken it, that she was addicted to crack cocaine, and she needed the money. In fact, she needed more. Patrick was stunned.

"Talk about culture shock!" *As I listen to him tell this his voice rises.* "This was my wife I had trusted? What a fool I was. How humiliating. After all, it was only my money she wanted. And I believed that she loved me and I wanted to be a good husband in the American way! But I will do it right next time."

I ask him what right is.

"Right is marrying a woman of your own tribe. I am going back to Nigeria at Christmas, and I will ask for the hand of a woman there that I know. She has many suitors but I think I will win over them all."

"How do you win?"

"With my money. In Nigeria, industry is valued above all things. You must not be lazy. Money proves you are not lazy and will be a good husband. Her parents will almost certainly choose me. The dowry will be about $10,000 and they will review my holdings."

"That seems like a lot of money."

"It is not so much. Ten thousand in Nigerian money is only about $1000 in the United States. And by the way, my parents must approve also. But there is no trouble because I am the oldest of seven children and I have provided for everyone. They cannot say no to me."

"I wish you well."

"You never know." *He hesitates.* "I know when I go back I could die anytime."

"What do you mean?"

"I only eat food my mother cooks, no other. People are envious of those who have wealth. They are suspicious too. They call on Juju and strange things happen. But if I die, I die and that's the way it is. I must live in my beautiful country in the ways that I know."

6
Conflict in the Dark Room

I seem to be
       Anne Frank
transparent
       as a branch in April
And I love.
       And have no need of phrases.
My need
       is that we gaze into each other.
How little we can see
       or smell!
We are denied the leaves,
       we are denied the sky.
Yet we can do so much—
       tenderly
embrace each other in a dark room.

—Yevgeny Yevtushenko
"Babii Yar"

Washington, D.C., 1942. *We hear the air raid sirens and have ten minutes to prepare for a half hour or maybe more of total darkness. Mother orders the five children to go to the bathroom and then to line up in the living room against the white, covered heater. She goes to the high cupboard and gets five Hershey bars saved for this occasion which she has purchased with precious rationing coupons. She hands us each one and tells us they must last the whole time. We hear the air raid warden's bell and the command, "Lights out!" Soon we huddle together in the darkness.*

Though at twelve years old I know this is a practice air raid, I am aware that at some point it may be real. In the dark, I think sober thoughts. They will hit Washington first, I think, because it is the hub of the world. They will get my dad because he works in Congress. If my dad had a chance, maybe he could fix the whole thing. He could say wait a minute, let's just talk things over. He would tell jokes. He would say how silly it is to kill each other and destroy houses. It is silly and I don't understand why one man like Hitler can make everybody do bad things. Why would he want to kill people like my friend Frieda Lipschitz?

My little brother gets restless and kicks me and I swat him back. Mother threatens to take away the rest of our candy bar if we aren't quiet. But mine is already gone. She feels around for him and pulls him onto her lap and begins to tell us Indian stories. How much longer, I ask when she is through. I am infinitely relieved when the all-clear sirens sound, the lights go on and my small world again seems civilized and safe and Frieda will still be there to play tomorrow.

Ancient Conflicts: Present Pain

We are discussing war after reading an essay on the subject by Jonathan Schell, and I am acutely aware that sitting in my class are a student from Israel and one from Lebanon.

David Eilat is a tall, young, pleasant Israeli with dark curly hair whose primary goal is to fly a plane in the Israeli air force. His father has spent twenty-seven years in the military in Israel and fought three major wars against the Arabs as commander of the forces on the West Bank. His father was forced to retire after a heart attack and now works for the Israeli government in the United States. David writes:

Israel has fought in 5 major wars with its Arab neighbors. All of them were caused by hatred, religion and disputes over territory. Today we have a new kind of war. They call it guerrilla warfare which is fought by terrorist organizations called Freedom Fighters. These groups hijack planes, put explosives in cars and drive them into buildings to kill innocent people. They capture and hold people hostage.

If this keeps going on in the future, wars will go on forever. If you've ever been in a war and made it out alive, you most likely will have nightmares and bad memories the rest of your life. My brother was a hero in the war in Lebanon but he has bad memories. In a war, nobody wins. I don't think peace will ever be achieved in my life time.

Ahmed-al-Housseini, of Lebanon, sits in the front row of the class.

David rises from his seat in the back to protest another student's negative comment about Israel. "If you had to deal with those murderers, you might feel like I do."

Ahmed looks down, then up, his face restrained and tense. He chooses silence.

*After class, I ask Ahmed if I may speak with him. "I am
concerned about David's remarks. I'm sure he meant no
offense to you personally."*

"It's O.K. I am used to it. I don't listen anymore and I won't
argue. If he knew what it's really like, he wouldn't say those
things."

*"I would like you to write about your experience in the Leba-
nese war."*

"That would be most difficult." *He paused, turned his head
away and then back.* "My mother was killed. They killed my
mother."

Ahmed writes:

April 13, 1975 at 6:00 o'clock in the morning, the civil war
between the Muslims and Christians began. My father said I
was not going to school that day, and I couldn't go for two
months. Every night we stayed in the basement because
shelling was not aimed against the fighters but against the
believers. We had no electricity, but used large quantities of
candles.

Days passed so slowly; we did not have anything to do.
Everyday we had bad news. All that was destroyable was
destroyed. Everyday about 100 people were taken; mothers, brothers, sisters, sons, daughters....

The business my father had built for fifteen years was
gone. We had no money. My mother continued to work for
that Italian paper but we did not see her frequently because
she had to be where the action was. The situation in all of
Lebanon got worse everyday.

At first the war was between Muslims and Christians. In
1978 Israel invaded Lebanon to get the Palestinians out of
the country because they were disturbing the security of
their northern borders. Then the Syrian army interfered

and everybody took advantage of that most beautiful country in the Middle East. In 1981, the Israeli army invaded Lebanon again.

During the invasions, my mother was in the south taking some pictures for her job. Some people were being tortured by the Israelis and she was taking pictures. They saw her and attacked and killed her. That was the end. I was 16 years old....

Lebanese Restaurant in Red

George Ayoub is an eager college freshman from Lebanon who wants to go to medical school. He has been in the United States three years and writes in his first essay about an experience with violence while he was working in a Lebanese restaurant.

On this particular afternoon, at about four o'clock, I was at work with my friends, Peter and Imad. We had four customers, our friends who had come in to give us a hard time and pick up something to eat. We were all standing around talking when it seemed the whole world came apart. With no warning, bombing and shelling began. The sounds of shells whistled above us and all around us. The explosions left our ears ringing, and the screams of people wounded and dying put terror into our souls. We didn't know what to do. We were running in all directions and into each other.

Peter, Imad and I grabbed Reema, one of our closest friends and hid in the cabinets to avoid flying glass from the windows and glasses. Our hearts were beating wildly as we hid. We didn't know who was fighting whom or where the battle was taking place. All we knew was that the rockets were all too close to our little restaurant.

The shelling lasted for seven hours. Shell after shell burst near us and finally about three o'clock in the morning, the big guns became silent. The shelling had stopped and we carefully came out of our hiding place. The girls were crying and screaming, and wanting to go home. So Peter and I decided to take them. We started to go outside and when we were just outside the door, a bomb exploded near by. We all quickly fell to the ground. We looked around, and no one, we thought, was injured, until Peter screamed. He had been hit in the knee by a piece of shrapnel.

I carried him inside and once again the girls started screaming. No one could gather enough courage to even go to the
bathroom to get a wet towel to put on the wound. We used
a dry towel.

We could still hear snipers shooting in the street, so we
decided to wait a little longer before trying to get out again.
We waited almost three hours until we couldn't hear any
more firing. Then we left to take Peter to the doctor and to
take the girls home.

Stories like this one have become the rule in Lebanon
today. My parents wanted me out of these dangerous situa-
tions, so they sent me to the United States. And I confess, I
wanted to be someplace a little safer myself.

It's Easy to Kill

Bassam Sleiman is in my office for his final interview for the semester. Sam (the American version of his name) has been here only two months from Lebanon and told me earlier of his desire to come to America to be an actor. "But that isn't the main reason," *he tells me.* "We came to escape the war. Our beautiful Beirut is torn apart. We don't know who our enemies are. The war is not between Lebanon and Muslims or Israel or Syria. It's all of them. You see, the middle of Beirut is Christian and Muslims are on either end. They kill you if you're Christian, which is what we are. Iraq pays mercenaries to kill Christians. Libyans offer 5,000 lire for a Christian head. So we set up defenses in cave churches. But one side is as bad as the other. There is so much hate. I have a Christian friend who, when he was fifteen years old, went to fight. That's what I'm going to write about in my last essay, in dialogue form. It's a true story. That fifteen-year-old boy is now going to school in Illinois."

Fouad (15-year-old boy as he enters a cave on the war front): Hi, sir.

Bchara: (35-year-old man): Hi, kid. Are you my partner?

Fouad: Yes, sir. They said you are the best and can teach me what to do.

Bchara: And right they did. I'm called Rambo around here. I've gunned down a whole army. I'm the best. And don't worry, just grab a machine gun and start killing.

Fouad: You mean...you mean kill people?

Bchara: You call those people? Listen, if you don't kill them they'll kill you, your mother, your father, your whole family. Take it from the best. It's easy to kill! That's my only lesson to you. Grab your gun and have some fun.

Bchara turned around and started shooting, laughing each time one of his enemies fell. Fouad hid behind a barrel and watched his maniac partner kill with pleasure. Then Bchara stopped shooting and looked at him.

Bchara: What are you looking at, kid? Grab your gun and start shooting. Look! There's nothing to it! Look! It's easy to kill! It's easy to kill! It's easy to kill! It's easy to kill!

He killed a man each time he said those words. Then he stopped, and pointed his gun toward Fouad.

Bchara: Fouad! You're next if you don't start shooting!

So Fouad grabbed his gun, aimed at a man, hesitated and didn't pull the trigger. Bchara yelled at him.

Bchara: Go ahead! It's easy to kill. Say it and shoot! It's easy to kill, it's easy to kill! I taught you all you need to know. Shoot! It's easy to kill!

Suddenly from the other side of the war ground, a bullet came screaming out of nowhere and pierced Bchara's head and threw him to the ground. Fouad threw his gun to the ground and ran toward Bchara. He held Bchara's head in his hands.

Fouad: There's something I have to say to you, sir.

Bchara looked up at him and said feebly: What?

Fouad: It's easy to *get* killed.

Bchara: You...you should have said that a little sooner, kid.

Untouchable

Monique Rahmani, a Kurdish woman from Iran with a doctorate in anthropology, sits at my table after lunch and tells me of her present predicament. A friend has introduced us; we discover our mutual interests and I invite her to my home.

In the California budget crunch, she has lost her job at San Diego State and has tried for four months to secure employment in the Los Angeles area. Her daughter, who completed her studies to become a physician in Iran, is unlicensed here and has been unable to find any job related to the medical profession in the area. This college professor tells me that at this point she "will do anything, clean houses, if necessary."

Monique does have an accent, but her English is flawless. Sometimes her voice is inaudible as she tells her story, her huge dark eyes occasionally glistening with moisture. Her face is expressionless, and her small body sags with heaviness. Yet there is a vestige of pride, something regal and self-contained in her manner that commands and rivets.

She and her daughter are out of money ("I have $30," she says) and have been told to leave the room they are subleasing in a two-bedroom apartment they share with a family of four. The landlord says it is too crowded but Monique says with a toss of her head, "I don't think that's it." She has tried to find another apartment but has been told several times it has already been rented when she knows it hasn't. She believes it is her accent. Even if it weren't, the first and last month's rent and a security deposit are always required which, given how exorbitant rental rates are, make it impossible in her situation.

Monique, as a young girl, married a wealthy nonpracticing Shiite Muslim, a Marxist and an atheist, who became an alcoholic. As a Kurd (a Sunni Muslim) Monique was considered untouchable by his Shiite family. When the couple lived

with the parents, the mother washed Monique's dishes sepa-
rately and wiped whatever she touched. She was considered
unclean. Her two children, a son and daughter, were unac-
ceptable also.

Monique's husband was in construction and they lived in a
huge house with marble floors, a chauffeur, maid, and cook,
but her husband abused both her and her children emotion-
ally and physically. She could see no way out of her marriage.
According to law, she could not divorce, nor could she have
custody of the children. She decided to go to school and eventually graduated from the university in Beirut with honors.

With great hope, she decided to make application for several
scholarships at American universities. Finally she was
awarded a stipend from Oklahoma State University at
Norman. With great temerity, she asked her husband if she
could go for a year to do graduate work, and to her sur-
prise, he said yes. She said she would be back, but knew she
wouldn't. With her children she made her escape from an
untenable situation and from the subsequent Iranian revolution. She says she has never regretted her decision.

She did tell her family that she was not coming back and
they thought she was crazy. Emigrating was unusual for a
man, but for a woman, the act was preposterous. Even her
brother, a well-educated, nonpracticing Muslim, begged her
not to go and with many tears cried, "Why do you do this?
You leave us. You leave the beautiful house and your many
possessions. Why?" The entire family wailed on her behalf.
Monique adds, "You have to understand that Iranians are
very emotional and excitable."

But she left, arrived safely in Oklahoma where she rented a
small apartment, and "felt peace for the first time in my
life." As a graduate student in anthropology with a linguis-
tics emphasis she excelled and continued her studies until
she was awarded a Ph.D. She secured a position at San
Diego State and was a visiting professor at UCLA.

Now she was close to being homeless.

Constanza

Constanza Wieczorek has just come from Poland to be an au pair and has enrolled in school to improve her English. Though she occasionally makes errors in sentence arrangement and word usage, she is bright and obviously a product of a stringent and well-founded educational system. She shares her thoughts about Auschwitz-Birkenau which is not far from her home in the outskirts of Warsaw, Poland:

I am Polish and the devastation and suffering caused by Hitler during World War II will stay in the memory of many generations. Our parents and grandparents still talk about those times as if they were yesterday. I do not even know my grandparents because they were killed during Poland's occupation by the German army.

Auschwitz-Birkenau has become a symbol of the martyrdom of the victims of Nazism. Built in 1940, it was the largest concentration camp in which more than 4,000,000 prisoners of 28 nationalities lost their lives, among them Polish intelligentsia, Soviet prisoners, homosexuals, Jehovah's Witnesses and a large number of Jews brought from all over Europe. The prisoners lived there in inhuman conditions, died in masses as a result of slave labor, hunger, illnesses, torture and executions. The corpses of the victims were burned in crematoriums or on pyres. Now there is a National Museum of Martyrology there. I think it gives the present generation a vision of what war is like.

Benjamin Franklin said, "There was never a good war, or a bad peace." History confirms that statement. There is no war without losses, dead soldiers, civilians, ruined cities, and orphaned children. I am a woman of peace and I hate wars, yet not at any cost. I cannot be indifferent to incidents where peace and freedom is taken away from innocent people. The peace of the world is the infinite treasure of all nations and it is the responsibility of every single citizen to make peace of ultimate value.

Constanza gives me a hug on the last day of school and hands me a small doll dressed in a traditional Polish dance costume to remember her by. She is going back to Poland in the summer but plans to return and perfect her English so she can become a translator.

I have my own encounter with Auschwitz ahead of me.

Work Brings Freedom

August 16, 1990. *Auschwitz-Birkenau, Poland. A fog rolls in and a mist covers the windows as our bus parks in the lot in front of the Auschwitz concentration camp. Over the entrance I read the doleful, ironic promise:* Arbeit Macht Frei *(Work Brings Freedom). We begin the tour with a guide whose English is so heavily accented and delivered in such a quiet monotone that we can barely understand. He keeps his head down and, in a strangely appropriate manner, speaks primarily with his eyes closed as he shows us rooms of human hair, shoes, personal effects, gas canisters, then grueling pictures, and anesthetizing statistics. The whole effect is numbing and I am glad to go outside and see small patches of green grass.*

We then go to the adjoining Birkenau, and I look with stunning familiarity at the bricked arch I had seen in so many movies, the one with the railroad tracks leading into the complex and the subsequent rows and rows of dormitories that remain, and I am astounded at the hugeness of this monstrosity, this scar on the face of mother earth. Only a few visitors, quiet and somber, bother to go see the pallets where the prisoners slept, bare wooden slats, side by side, covered with hay. We go along with a Jewish doctor on our tour who has made this pilgrimage to visit the country of his progenitors, two of whom survived this camp. We notice, as we walk, a well-dressed family speaking in Hebrew, wandering among the buildings, looking and searching. The Jewish doctor tells us what this family is saying. It seems the father was in Birkenau as a young boy, and he is looking for the number of the pallet where he slept.

The man is composed and matter-of-fact, narrating to his family, a grown son and daughter, as they explore. All at once, he identifies his sleeping place, which he points out. As they look, he suddenly stops talking, breaks down, and falls to his knees, sobbing. After a few moments, his son gently lifts him up and leads him away.

Hungarian Refugee

Erzsebet Vrabel from Budapest, Hungary, announces the first day, "Don't ask me to talk because I don't speak English very good." *Yet she has a perfect score on her diagnostic grammar exam and seems to socialize freely with her fellow students.*

My most shameful experience happened to me in Austria. It is a unique story, but the feeling of shame must be familiar to everyone.

I spent two years in Austria as a refugee from my home in Budapest, Hungary. The refugee camp was in a little town next to Vienna, the capital of Austria. For having a little entertainment, just for wandering around the city, we had to take a train. Many times the refugees didn't have tickets on their trips, especially when they just arrived from the country, where they had fled from.

The Austrians hated us because we didn't speak their language. We were loud strangers, troublemakers in their sunny, tranquil lives.

Once I and three friends of mine got to the train at the end station. The train was almost empty. The conductor came and asked for our tickets. When he got them he tore them to pieces and he went away. We were shocked but still we hoped. He knew that we had tickets. On the next station he called another conductor, big like a gorilla, and they told us to leave the train because we didn't have tickets. In our poor language knowledge we tried to save our rights, but they grabbed us and they threw us down from the train. I was crying, the others were crying too, but only inside. I saw hate in their eyes. The shame poured over us.

Erzsebet writes another essay about her father:

My father is lovable for me, even if we were submitted to some humiliating events because of him. His heritage was a cause for some people to treat us unjustly. I sometimes heard the whispering words, "because he is a gypsy" which is insulting in Hungary. It means that someone is uncivilized, unable to progress, primitive, lives in a tent whose only recognized arbiter is the knife. My Daddy was neither uncivilized or primitive, but he had black hair and black eyes and a vagabond nature. When my sister wanted to get married, the parents of her lover were frightened by the possibility of gypsy-looking grandchildren. All of us felt shame and were helplessly crying. Do we think enough about looking at the other's inner world rather than their outward appearance? We all have sensitive souls and we do not like being hurt by prejudice.

Life with Only Chopin

Bogumila Lowery has been here about three years from Warsaw, Poland. She married an American man, subsequently divorced, and is now living alone. All her family are still in Poland. She writes:

I turned on the radio and there was no news, no talk shows, nothing but our beloved Chopin, Chopin and more Chopin. On December 16, 1981 at 6:00 o'clock a.m., General Jaruzelski announced on Polish television the "imposition of a state of war." All Solidarity buildings were seized, most of the leadership was rounded up at Gdansk by riot police. There were mass arrests throughout Poland as tanks and armored vehicles poured out into the streets. All the telephone and cable links with the outside world were cut. The active civilian telephone network was disconnected and a curfew was imposed.

All the cinemas, theaters and all public activities were shut down. We could not travel to other cities, only with special permission for things like a funeral or visiting somebody very rich. Not even one museum or gallery was open.

In Warsaw on every corner you could see soldiers, not only Polish but Russian. It was a horrible feeling. One Russian tank carried a huge advertisement of the movie, *Apocalypse Now,* showing a horrible picture of mutilated bodies.

The most depressing experience was to not be able to meet people and talk with them. So many of us lost jobs and did not have contact with each other. Throughout the city and even throughout all the country was emptiness and cold, a country with one thousand years of history, a country with so much faith in freedom and a better life.

General Jaruzelski insisted that he had acted to prevent a "national catastrophe" and that this was a course of reform and renewal. It was such a sad history lesson for all of us in Poland. Little by little, restrictions were removed and martial law finally ended in July 1983 after a second papal visit to Poland. From that time on, I recognized music by Chopin very easily—the only music played on the radio during martial law.

February 1989. *I can only guess how I might feel as a stranger in a new country, learning a new language and unusual ways, or how desolate life might be without family support. I confess to myself that there are many students I would like to take home with me. It is then I am acutely aware of my limitations, of the brief shot I have at these students to make any difference at all. One semester and they are gone, or sooner if they are discouraged. Futility sets in. I want them to know the possibilities.*

August 1974. *My oldest son, at nineteen, will leave soon to go to Germany for two years and immerses himself in the study of the language and culture. The day before he is to leave we assemble as a family to celebrate our twenty-second anniversary, planned by the children. We know it will be our last night together as a family.*

The four teenagers blindfold my husband and me and we tacitly submit as they take us in separate cars to an unknown destination over unfamiliar roads. The car stops, they help me out, walk me through sand so I'm sure we're at the beach, but when they take off the blindfold I find it's only a sandbox. We've arrived at the local park. My husband is already seated at a card table, covered with a lace cloth, set with china, crystal, and candles.

Happy Anniversary! All of them wait on the table and serve us an elegant meal, hors d'oeuvres to dessert. Entertainment follows. Eric, Craig, Lisa, Susan, Robin, and our Indian daughter, Frankie, climb up on the wooden platform in the play area and perform—singing, dancing, telling jokes. Then the climax. Eight-year-old Robin pulls out her violin and begins to play the melody of what has become our family song: "Edelweiss." The wavery notes sound out, slurring and sliding on the night air. And this time no one laughs; our imperfections bond us and we are acutely aware of our own vulnerability.

Eric then sings the song in German and we all join in on the last verse. By that time, my husband and I are on the platform too, and at the end of the song we become one hugging, teary mass—one of those moments where differences are forgotten, where happy eclipses sad and there is unity and wholeness.

Even in the family, polarities are with us. The pull is constant in any group between unity and variety, between the individual and the relationship, between happy and sad, between the ideal and the reality. In fact, these small units are essentially macrocosmic worlds, where the inherent tension creates energy but also an ominous volatility. But this tension is tolerable if there are moments of coming together, and the memories of those occasions give us hope they will happen again.

7
Possibilities

Ethnic distinctions do not depend on an absence of social interaction and acceptance, but are, quite to the contrary, often the very foundations on which embracing social systems are built. Interaction in such social systems does not lead to its liquidation through change and acculturation; cultural differences can persist despite inter-ethnic contact and interdependence.

—Fredrik Barth
Ethnic Groups and Boundaries

Love in Lagos

Mowell Obonyano of Lagos speaks in the typical, rolling African accent with traces of British English and often must repeat his contributions to the discussions so we can understand. He is perceptive, humane, with an honesty that often brings laughter. The class comes to expect his responses. In fact, I sense they wait for him to lead. When we talk about defining abstractions like love, he raises his hand and says, "I know what love is because my father had three wives." Laughter sweeps the class; eyebrows raise; the student next to Mowell slaps him on the back. He writes:

I'm from a family of twenty-one children and the only thing that kept the family together was love. My father is chairman of our town organization and is known for his charisma and the persuasive way he solves family matters. Of the four most important things in life: money, education, security and family, we lacked three of the above essential factors. But we had a great family and this is where I learned about love.

In my country, it's O.K. to have more than one wife and my father had three. Of the twenty-one children in the family, my mother had only three and I was the last born of the three. My mother died two years after my birth. So I was raised by my first stepmother. She was like a real mother to me because of the way she loved and cared for me, sometimes even more than her own children. She had eleven children of her own.

I missed her very much when she left Lagos to live in Bendel, where she managed my father's new business. After she left, I lived with my second stepmother who had seven children and also treated me like one of her own. I was the only child that was raised by three mothers. I never felt bad for one day about having been raised by stepmothers, because it was like being raised by my own mother. My family taught me what love really is.

Is Love, Like Real?

Diane Southwood, blond, cherub-faced, sits on the lab table in front of the classroom (our room is in the chemistry department) and waits after class until everyone is gone.

"Have you read my essay yet, the one on love?"

"Yes, I have." Diane is getting married in three months, so I'm not surprised she chooses this topic to practice writing about abstractions.

"What do you think?"

"I think in your essay that love still remains an abstraction. You have some good thoughts, maybe even profound ideas, but you need examples or perhaps a fresh metaphor, some attachment to experience to make it more concrete."

Diane sighs. "Love is pretty abstract. Pretty mysterious. And nobody seems to know what it is. Especially married love."

"You might try limiting your topic to this idea of romantic love."

Diane goes on as if I did not make the last comment. "Like my mom or like anybody when I ask about love and marriage they laugh or make jokes or whatever. I think there's some big secret about this. Something they're not telling me. Maybe love just goes away. Is love, like real?"

I think we're getting into heavy stuff—the whole European courtly love tradition—this pervasive Western idea of marrying for love—the volatile contemporary fashion of marriage as "out," and now marriage as "in"—the simplicity of the idea of sex as an end in itself ("What's Love Got to Do with It?").

My mind races over the data and I stop on the word "acculturation." Another student, Shivani from India, has known since she was a child who had been chosen as her husband by her parents—group values over individual choice. Here in the West love is all, seriously pursued by the self-defined looking for Jung's perfect anima/animus to fill the emptiness. Love? The Universal Definition isn't there. The Greeks' Agape is the impossible ideal, and married love seems to ground itself in the utilitarian, somewhere in the fog of bills, dirty diapers, and crabgrass. But everybody wants love and sex together. And we want it to go on forever.

I've been married thirty-five years and should be able to put aside the study of English Literature and converse intelligently about my first profession. But I feel like a mushmouth. Be specific and concrete now. Is love, like real?

"I hope so," I hear myself say to her. "You know, we may be in for a long session here. I tell you what, I'll just give you my experience and observations. But remember, yours may be different."

"O.K., that's great. I just want to know."

We talk at length and she leaves, perhaps not older and wiser but ready to test my experience against hers.

I think of what is possible. Lines from T. S. Eliot jump-start my thoughts:

> See, now they vanish,
> The faces and places, with the self which, as it could, loved
>   them
> To become renewed, transfigured, in another pattern.

I want to write about it but I need more time. When the semester is over, I have an operation. While convalescing I write:

Is Love, Like Real?

> Asks the young girl about to be married
> is there something they're not telling me?
> All married people when I ask advice sigh look away
> tell me to always keep communication going
> are not joyful in their smiling
> their talk like the babble of a balloon losing air
> Is love, like real?

I think of a poem I wrote long ago: Love Is a Unicorn
which I did not believe, clearly was a defense
against disappointment but today light-years away
a story has been writing itself beginning when I was,
in years 18 (B.C.) before college before carnal before children
before consciousness when I asked: what is love?
love was my father someone just like him in every way
except more like Errol Flynn and I was Marian in Robin Hood
with a cone hat hung with yards of amorphous veiling

so when I was eighteen after my appendectomy
and felt a hand take mine hold a barf pan for me in the other
I didn't recognize *him*
was only embarrassed to be common and without makeup
him in his football sweater and all besides he didn't dance
you see, the cultural crust on my brain covered the neocortex
which always covers the "old" brain, the reptilian one
so how could I know with all these veils on?
But nevertheless I followed the prescribed pattern did everything
a perfect Western White Christian daughter would do
my wedding cake was decorated with real roses
my grandmother embroidered fig leaves on an apron for me

I thought I knew when children came and went,
passing like dreams joy quiet and hard to catch
as the blown white heads of dandelions
love children want all the time short bursts aren't enough
but man and woman?
we aren't even related how can I love him when he snores
is painfully provincial never quite knows what I mean
And lust? Lust is a chemist who boils us together
or conjures dreams of Charlton Heston whose feet,
I found out later are, well, flat
incredible these veils such demons dance in front of knowing

today again in this hospital bed I woke and saw his knee
how long had he been there hours no thirty years
he didn't sleep or snore he cradled the kidney pan under my chin
and stayed to empty the bile again again in all these years how
many times was he dancing as he emptied it?
how blessedly provincial

then I felt the wedding band smooth across my wet forehead
as he pushed back my hair
and as he did, something passed from his hand to my head
something powerful insistent pierced clear through
the triune brain, through to the very core that never lies
and clearly I heard the whisper yes
and I slept.

Forgiveness

*Antonio Perez-Cordoba, from Mexico City, is a small, dapper
man nearly forty who will graduate from the university with
a degree in psychology as soon as he passes his writing
requirements. He wants extra practice, and I suggest he
write an essay on a subject of his choice. He selects "Forgiveness" as a topic and I ask what he has in mind as a main
idea.*

"You will see."

"Can you give me an idea?"

"I have a specific incident I will write about."

"Then this will be primarily a narrative."

"A story. Yes."

"Will it be like a talk you might give in church?"

"Oh no. I don't belong to any church. I plan to study forgiveness as therapeutic in the treatment of mental disease."

The next week he brings his essay.

About five years ago I was living in Mexico City with my
wife and children and working in a clerking job at an office
to earn money to come to the United States. I was providing
money for my father and mother also, so I could not save
very much. But after two and a half years I had $200! Soon
we would be ready to take the bus to Los Angeles. I brought
the money to work because I thought I would go see how
much the tickets cost. I put it in an envelope and in a
drawer in the back of my desk.

When I went to get it, it was gone. I asked, but no one in the
office knew about it. The only person who could possibly
know was a friend I worked with. I knew from the way he
acted that he took it. He didn't hang around anymore and I

knew it was him. But he would not admit it. Later he did, but he had spent all the money and could not pay it back.

All my savings were gone and I would have to work another two and a half years! I became very bitter and angry. This anger affected my whole life. I was not a patient father and husband. I was miserable to live with and mad at everybody. I could hardly live with myself. The world seemed very black.

One day I was walking on the street and stopped at a newspaper stand and bought a paper from a man with shabby clothes. The man greeted me in such a friendly way that I was impressed to ask him why he was so happy. He gave a quiet answer: "Because I have forgiven the world."

I thought about his words all day. I decided to try it. I would completely forgive this friend. So the next day I went to work and asked him to come in the office. He was scared because he thought I would turn him over to the law but instead I said, "I want you to know I forgive you completely. I know you needed the money. You do not have to pay me back. I will take you to a fine dinner to prove that I forgive you."

He was surprised and didn't quite believe me. But we went to a nice restaurant and I really tried to put my anger out of my mind. I would not only forgive, I would forget. He had a relieved look on his face.

My whole life changed; I became a different person. My wife told me I even looked different. Somehow I saved the money faster than I thought I could and with what I borrowed from an uncle I was able to come to the United States in one year.

I saw the power of forgiveness and what it did to my mind. So I want to study about this act and what it can do to those with great anger in their hearts.

After three semesters and much hard work, Antonio passes the writing exam.

He says he wants to repay me in some way for my help and asks me to come to his home and have a Mexican lunch prepared by his wife. I tell him he doesn't have to do this, that his thanks is enough. However, he asks twice again and insists I would honor him greatly if I would come.

So I go to his small apartment to meet his family, two daughters, Isis and Ishtar, and his wife, Rosa, who does not speak English. She smiles a great deal as she sets out what must be the best of all she has and prepares a picture-perfect meal. I see the table is only set for two. Antonio motions for me to sit and when I ask where his wife and children will sit he tells me they will go into the bedroom and stay so we can have a quiet meal. I protest. He insists this is the way it is done and that she will not mind.

I hear them in the bedroom as she desperately tries to keep the children quiet. I tell him I cannot be comfortable in this situation and ask if he would allow them to come out. Begrudgingly, he does. The wife and children do not eat what we have but snack on the donuts I brought.

Antonio is accepted into graduate school in another state with a full scholarship and finds a mentor interested in his research on the influence of forgiveness on the human psyche.

September 1989. *We read the short story "A & P" by John Updike, a venerable rite-of-passage story in which a young man quits his job as a grocery store checker on a matter of principle—because he is incensed by the treatment of three young girl customers.*

The class responds: "A stupid story. Why would anyone quit a job for three girls they didn't know?" "This doesn't make sense." "I'm sure his parents would be mad if he quit his job." "He's a geek."

I am amazed that they miss the point altogether. I cogitate. Obviously, financial security to this group is of more importance than the defense of a nebulous principle. I am reminded that if basic needs are not satisfied, ethical and aesthetic issues are secondary.

I subsequently select the fiction and poetry I use with a greater awareness. But I don't abandon my favorites altogether because I was conditioned by a shamelessly idealistic father who, in the midst of the overwhelming challenge of my young mother's extended illness and death, took me to art galleries, sang silly love songs, and spun tales at breakfast that made oatmeal taste like ambrosia.

I remember a poem my father quoted so often that for years I thought he wrote it:

> If of thy mortal goods thou art bereft,
> And from thy slender store two loaves alone
> to thee are left,
> Sell one, and with the dole,
> Buy hyacinths to feed thy soul.
>
> —Saadi (thirteenth-century Persian poet)

The Geode

Estrella Mendez is about twenty years old, heavyset, pock-marked, speaks to no one, and sits in the back of the class-room. In an interview she tells me about her shyness, says she worries about speaking "right" and mostly enjoys tend-ing children rather than associating with her peers. She writes about her most memorable Christmas:

It was midnight December 24, 1986, my first Christmas here in the United States. I felt so lonely, like I was all by myself even when I was surrounded by others. I was in a restaurant with my uncle, cousin and other friends and we were having dinner when midnight arrived.

I had to go out of the restaurant, I wanted to cry so bad. When I was out, my cousin came up to me and asked if I was O.K. I told him that I felt so lonely and I wished I could be with my mom and family in Guatemala.

He hugged me and told me that if I wanted to, cry because it would do a lot of good for me. I started crying, remem-bering the Christmas in Guatemala. They were so different than here. In Guatemala we make special kinds of food and have firecrackers at midnight. This is a tradition we have. And everything was still and silent. Most of all I missed my family. This was the saddest and loneliest Christmas I ever had.

Ashamed of My Mom

Sean Ramstead, a California sun-bleached blond surfer-type, says as he introduces himself the first day of class, "I don't know anybody in this school." I ask how many are in the same situation and three-fourths of the students raise their hands.

I assign the first essay—a strong experience from early childhood. Sean comes up after class and tells me he's not a good writer and he can't remember anything about his childhood that's worth writing about. I ask him if he felt strongly about anyone in his childhood. He answers a tentative yes.

"Then describe that person and tell an experience you had with him or her," I suggest.

He stands there looking pained.

I add, "Don't worry about being a 'good' writer. Just write what you feel and then edit later."

"Somebody I feel strongly about...?" *He shuffles out the door without further comments. His paper is the first on my desk the next class period.*

When I was a little boy I was ashamed of my Mom. Although she is a very pretty, loving, caring, happy and smart person, I was ashamed because she cleans houses.

I was ashamed because other students at school would ask me what my mom did or somehow it would come up in conversation. They would say, all surprised, "Your mom's a maid?" It bothered me then but now I know better and it's fine with me.

When my sister and I were young my mom and dad lived in an apartment. They were just teenagers. My dad worked at a grocery store and my mom took care of us. My dad wouldn't let my mom work or go to school or anything. Then they got divorced and my mom had to go out and clean houses so she could take care of us. She's a great person. I owe her a lot.

My mom still cleans houses, but she went back to school and she just got her bachelor's degree after ten years of going to school. She's 39 years old and starting over, or maybe just starting. I love my mom more than life itself.

Flight from North Korea: My Father's Story

Paul Lee, who emigrated with his family from Korea five years ago, has spoken only once in class. In our discussion about violence, he briefly stated, without commentary, that his uncle's business was destroyed in the riots and that there was no money to rebuild it. In response to an essay assignment on families he writes:

It was dawn and my father had to get up early to search for food for his family. It was a cold and windy morning and he was only ten years old. He and his family were refugees from North Korea to South Korea traveling on foot and on the train. They were fleeing from the North because Soviet communism was taking over. Their destination was the South, though they did not have any friends or relatives who lived in South Korea.

His shirt was torn apart; one shoe was gone. Every town they went through was discovered in ashes. The houses were empty; they had also gone South. He went into the houses searching for food or goods left but there wasn't any.

Then he saw something in the yard that was covered with dirt. He dug for it, and found a sack filled with rice, about 80 pounds. The sack was heavier than he was, but with all his energy, he carried it to his family and they had a good rice dinner.

This was my Dad's story when I asked him about his child-hood. After I heard it, I went to McDonald's to get a bite of hamburger.

Why I Love Being Italian

November 1991. *Donna Salatino walks toward the school cafeteria, with fashionable holes in the knees of her tight jeans, her dark hair teased and moussed into an aura of disarray. She approaches me as I walk toward her.*

"About that paper. On my culture? I wrote it already but I think it's all wrong. You know that word you wrote on the board, that ethno-something word?"

"Ethnocentrism?"

"Yeah, that's it. Well, I think I did that on my paper. That ethnocentrism you told us about. See, I wrote about how being an Italian is so much better than being an American. Like comparing—and now that I think about it, it was a real put-down. When I wrote it I thought, I hope she doesn't ask me to read this in class."

"What if you just describe your own feelings? Tell what you love about being Italian. In fact, you might title your essay, "What I Love About Being Italian."

"That's better, isn't it? I mean, even when you have an argument with somebody you're not supposed to attack the person—just describe how you're feeling. I learned that in psychology."

"Right. You don't need to do a comparison/contrast. Now tell me some of the things you love about being Italian."

"Well, I really am crazy about pasta—all the way. And pas-·sion! We just say what we feel. I hate blaa. Life is up and down, never blaa beige. I think I can develop it pretty well. Well, thanks a lot. I gotta go to class."

8
We Are All Related

There are birds of many colors—
red, blue green, yellow—yet it is all
one bird. There are horses of
many colors—brown, black, yellow,
white—yet it is all one horse. So
cattle, so all living things—animals,
flowers, trees. So men: in this
land where once were only Indians
are now men of every color—
white, black, yellow, red—
yet all one people.

—Hiamove, Chief among the Cheyenne and the Dakotas
In *Indians' Book*
by N. Curtis

An Indian Son

August 1967. *Through a social service agency, we arrange to be foster parents to a Navajo boy from Shadow Mountain, Arizona. We see him get off the bus in new jeans and cowboy hat; he is short for his twelve years, diffident and cocky, yet with some small, unmistakable terror in his eyes. He stands head down as introductions are made, and when I give him an obligatory hug he is stiff and unyielding.*

He is painfully quiet and seems miserable. I am frustrated, feeling foolish, like an overbearing Lady Bountiful, and think of a quote from a Yeats poem, "...the worst are full of passionate intensity." I leave him alone and wait for him to come to us.

When he thinks I am not looking he feels the refrigerator, strange to him, wondering why it is not cold on the outside too. In his room, he pats the mattress and I find later he is used to sleeping on a Navajo rug in a tent, or out on the desert. Lights are a source of wonderment; running water and suds are playthings—he becomes the official washer of dishes. When we go anywhere, he will not let me walk ahead, but periodically turns slyly back to see where I am going.

My son reports that Reynolds takes one of my paring knives to school tucked in his sock on the first day of school and I realize he does not know what to expect. He evidently establishes his ground, for no one will bother him and he is no further trouble. He begins to smile a lot but still his words are few.

He becomes brave and though he will not do the Eagle Dance because he has no costume, he sings part of the Navajo night chant on a school program. He chants softly, with tones that slip and slide between intervals.

Happily may I walk.
Happily, with abundant dark clouds, may I walk.
Happily, with abundant showers, may I walk.
Happily, with abundant plants, may I walk.
Happily, on a trail of pollen, may I walk.
Happily may I walk.
Being as it used to be long ago, may I walk.
May it be beautiful before me,
May it be beautiful behind me,
May it be beautiful below me.
May it be beautiful above me,
May it be beautiful all around me.
In beauty it is finished.

*He is shy and sits down quickly, playing with the silver
squash blossom necklace on his chest. Soon he will go home.
I write:*

To My Indian Son Leaving for
the Reservation

Child of Shadow Mountain
Coyote brother of the desert. Son.
Slip your brown hand away
A dark-haired mother waits.

Bareback you rode into our saddled lives
How far from here to there?
A white skin and a century away
Somehow we bridged the gap.

We wove you
In the fabric of our lives.
The pattern will be rent
'Til you return.

*He returns in the fall and the following summer we visit him
on the reservation. Reynolds has told us they move with the
sheep so when we arrive, we go to his grandfather's hogan
after receiving directions from the trading post.*

We travel in the dust and sagebrush and finally see his grandfather, lean and wizened, bare to the waist, stirring a pot on a tripod. He calls off the barking dogs and we show him Reynolds's picture and ask him where the family camp is. He knows what we ask and draws a map in the sand, explaining the directions in Navajo. We stand, abject in our stupidity, and he impatiently erases the map with a stick and waves us on. He was our only contact so we start back to the trading post.

We see another hogan along our way, so we drive the van over the sagebrush and park. The smell hits twenty feet away, but we keep walking toward the dirt/log shelter. Three people sit outside, so we ask if they know where the Seschille family might be. A man staggers to his feet and comes toward us, glassy-eyed and incoherent. Two obese women in traditional Navajo dress are propped against the wall of the hogan in a stupor; flies crawl around their eyes and noses. Rags soaked with paint lie beside them and we know. We retreat quickly, mumbling apologies lost in the dust of our footsteps.

Only with a guide from the trading post who leads us over the interminable sagebrush do we find his family. In the distance over a little rise, we see a tent and sheep grazing. A woman walks among the sheep and children play around the entrance. As we approach the camp, everyone disappears inside the tent and we are left to wonder what to do next.

I go to the entrance with a picture of Reynolds and lift the flap of the tent. The mother is crouched on the corner of a bare mattress holding her baby with fear in her eyes. A carcass of mutton hangs from the underpinnings of the tent, and the only furnishings I can see are the mattress and several cardboard boxes. She is in the traditional Navajo velvet bodice and long, tiered skirt; the baby is in a cloth diaper only.

I show Reynolds's picture; she smiles broadly, stands and comes toward me, speaking in Navajo. Just then we hear a horse and Reynolds rides into the camp through the sheep. He seems glad at first to see us but sinks into embarrassment and runs away for a while.

We stay the night in our van, and in the morning I watch through the window. I feel the sage, the sun, the sheep, turquoise on velvet, timelessness, something primal, close to earth yet like the shape of holiness. I write:

> From the tent she came,
> a wrinkled butterfly in blue and purple velvet
> hair wound up with rags
> and stood before the desert's morning grey.
> Sheep crackled in the sage
> and she, moving among them put each lamb
> to its mother's teat,
>
> poured water from a can into an iron pot
> hung on a tripod built a fire beneath it
> timeless her wrist her life her earth her bodice
> held together loosely with pins over bare breasts;
> she watched the horses steam the air
> untethering them to run toward the river.
>
> An infant came toddling from the tent;
> she sat down at the stoop velvet
> falling between her legs,
> and he came, lifted her blouse,
> milk squirting on his face as he found her nipple.
> And I, watching from the van marveled
>
> at what is first and last simple and holy
> yet like a feather caught in cactus
> blown and lost in the east wind.
> Now in my sight a hawk circles the dawn
> then stuns his prey; a mouse
> caught in his beak writhes furiously
> against a destiny of sacrifice.

Reynolds grows up, decides to stay home to go to high school. He marries a Navajo girl and names his first son after my first son.

An Indian Daughter

September 1972. *Frances Marie Williams, a Pima from Coolidge, Arizona, comes to live with us.*

Frankie's short black hair is profuse, bluntly cut around a broad face lit with a smile that reveals rows of perfect teeth and draws us easily to her. She is well-built, almost stocky, with the natural, open, unaffected manner of a fourteen-year-old girl.

The second day she jumps on the back of my fifteen-year-old son, throws him to the floor and proceeds to sit on him with good-natured triumph. We are all amused, but Frankie and I talk privately about these things that might be misinterpreted by a less tolerant or perhaps less naive young man.

"O.K.," *she laughs at herself.*

As we talk, I am ironing and she stands leaning against the cabinet. For a few seconds it is quiet except for the plop of the iron. Then she speaks quickly.

"You know, I want to do well in school. I'm really going to make something of myself." *Her energy seems to gather with the force of the years taken to make these words.* "You'll see. I'm going to graduate from college."

Her vehemence surprises and delights me and I want to believe her. Yet her education has been substandard; her childhood in a family of fourteen children of alcoholic parents in a severely economically depressed situation has been traumatic. Frankie tells me her sister was raped on the way home from church by four white men who were arrested, then released the next day. They lived in a tenuous atmosphere of insecurity and prejudice in the small town bordering the reservation; they and those like her were almost nonpersons.

June 1974. *Frankie graduates from South High School, Torrance, California. The night before, I walk in the bedroom to check in on Lisa and Frankie before I go to bed. On either side of the room they are asleep in twin beds, these inseparable sisters. My daughter's long blond hair spills over the covers and Frankie's long black hair over hers, and I stand there knowing I am viewing wholeness, a bright moment akin to experiencing art, a coming together that somehow makes life tolerable.*

May 1980. *Today we attend Frankie's university graduation. Frankie has married Kelly Harris, a Catawba from South Carolina, in her senior year and has a reception at my mother's home with entertainment by the Intertribal Choir in full costume. And today, as she graduates with a degree in education, she walks across the stage, black hair flowing beneath her cap and eight months' pregnant. She names her first girl Lisa after my daughter.*

June 1991. *Frankie has three children, teaches school on the Catawba reservation, and her husband, who is a speech therapist, also works at night ushering in a movie theater so they can meet expenses. The tribe has no cultural center, no "powwow" and is considered in sociological studies to be completely assimilated into the dominant culture.*

Marie

August 1982. *Marie Curley, a Navajo from the reservation near Page, Arizona, comes to live with us. She is a tall, flirtatious, and uncharacteristically garrulous girl who does well in school.*

Though she receives from the tribe an athletic scholarship to the university, in her senior year of high school she becomes pregnant after going home to the reservation for Christmas. She marries a Navajo man and has two children. He becomes an alcoholic, they divorce, and he eventually commits suicide in front of his children. She gets a job in a factory where her face is badly burned in an industrial chemical accident. Eventually, Marie gets her high school degree at night and finds a job working with computers for the Bureau of Indian Affairs. She writes in January 1991:

I'm proud to be an American Indian. It's what I am and always will be. It makes me lift my head up high and strive for the best, even when things get tough. I'm also proud of my ancestors of what they've gone through, like my great-great grandpa who died on the Long Walk of the Navajos. I'm proud to live and proud to die.

Most white people think of Indians as second class level still. I have been treated like that before. It's not a good feeling. Just because most Indians are uneducated, doesn't mean we don't know nothing. Believe me, we're a lot smarter in our own ways. I usually turn around and give them my point of view to let them know not to judge me for my heritage or color.

But sometimes I'm ashamed to be an Indian, because in Page or over in Gallup, there's a lot of alcoholics just staggering around the streets. They make me look cheap, especially when I see them begging for money from the tourists. No wonder they look down on us. It's not all the Indians,

just the drunks around town. But the white man first introduced alcohol to the Indians. Now that's all most Indians
want these days.

Sometimes I'm made fun of for the way I talk. It used to
bother me, but not anymore. I look at it as I speak two
languages, and if they think I sound funny, let them think
that way. I'm proud for who I am. It's just that I speak more
Navajo than English.

I want my children to grow up with pride and respect for
who they are and have them appreciate life.

This is my true soul and feelings in words. I am who I am
and who I said I was. I am the image of myself. I am Indian.

*Marie makes necklaces of juniper berries and beads for
every member of my class in Native-American Literature at
CSUDH and gives me the wedding basket used in her Navajo
marriage ceremony.*

.

Dancing Leaf

January 1991. *I begin my class in Native-American Literature and Contemporary Problems. After class, outside the door, a young woman encounters me, breathless and animated, her light curly hair disheveled and her eyes bright behind heavy lenses.*

"Hi! I'm Lisa Duckworth. I couldn't make it today, but I want to take your class. My mother is French and my father is Cherokee and I was raised on the reservation. I'm so glad they're offering this class."

"Great. You can give it to us straight."

"My Indian name is Dancing Leaf—just so you will know when I sign the roll."

We begin with Momaday's House Made of Dawn *and go on to Silko's* Ceremony. *Lisa reads and understands in a way no one in the class can. Dancing Leaf (we call her that now) knows about this power and beauty of words; she sees the whole, a world where earth and sky, people and animals, word and action are not separate.*

She tells us about her childhood on the Cherokee reservation in the 1960s where her father made her wear buckskins to school. She describes the sacred pipe ceremony as well as the peyote rites as they are still practiced. She tells us the Cherokee versions of several legends and reads from Silko:

> I will tell you something about stories,
>> (he said)
> They aren't just entertainment.
>> Don't be fooled,
> They are all we have, you see,
>> all we have to fight off
>>> illness and death.

152

You don't have anything
if you don't have stories.
        Their evil is mighty
but it can't stand up to our stories
let the stories be confused or forgotten
        They would like that
        They would be happy
Because we would be defenseless then.

        He rubbed his belly.
        I keep them here
        (He said)
        Here, put your hand on it

        See, it is moving.
        There is life here
        for the people.

And in the belly of this story
the rituals and the ceremony
        are still growing.

        What she said:

        The only cure
        I know
        is a good ceremony
That's what she said. (1977, 2-3)

*At the conclusion of the class, we have an American Indian
dinner at my home. Lisa does a Cherokee blessing and
purification ceremony for us, in English, she says, so we can
understand.*

*All fifteen of us go outside and form a circle while she stands
in the center with a bowl of different varieties of dried herbs
in smoking coals. She gives each of us a pheasant feather,
keeping one for herself. She directs the smoke from the bowl
with her feather up "toward heaven," she says, so that this
prayer will be heard. She turns to each point of the compass
and says a different prayer/blessing at each turn. She
blesses the "two-leggeds" and "four-leggeds," the earth*

*above, below and around us, the growing things that nour-
ish us and give us clothing and warmth, the good and the
evil in all things. Then she blesses each of us as we, with the
feather, brush the smoke toward us as a gesture of purification. She instructs us to all join hands and to silently medi-
tate for a moment.*

*No one laughs or seems to feel uncomfortable. Something
primal and simplistic, compelling and cleansing happens,
and we begin our meal and spend our evening more aware
of the human need for unity with each other and the natural
world, aware of some insouciant pull toward that which is
unsayable.*

June 1991, Last day of the semester. *My class at Harbor College plans a potluck lunch, and I hand back their writing portfolios and journals. Grading is my least favorite task. Though I make my grading criteria clear, I still find exceptions, qualifications, mitigating circumstances. Many of these people have been categorized and put in boxes all their lives. The arbitrariness grates; the one little mark I make on the computerized grade sheet says so little and means so much. I write a personal note in each folder to justify myself and hope I have not done permanent damage.*

I assess myself as I assess them, and I seriously wonder how many of them will be happy and successful. Are they just shadows in a shadowed world? Yet, on this last day, I dutifully smile, relieved to be through with this semester, feeling like I've given it my best shot.

I am thinking seriously that I don't have to do this; maybe this will be my last semester. I could play tennis. I could write. I could sleep in.

But after a couple of weeks I am rested, and a quote from Tennyson's "Ulysses" that I memorized in college digs into my psyche:

> 'Tis not too late to seek a newer world
> . . . .
> Tho' much is taken, much abides; and
>   tho'
> We are not now that strength which in old
>   days
> Moved earth and heaven; that which we are,
>   we are;
> One equal temper of heroic hearts,
> Made weak by time and fate, but strong in
>   will
> To strive, to seek, to find, and not to yield.

The old Rocky *theme—a response perhaps too dramatic for a homely decision, but I know that for now, I want to teach. Perhaps I need them more than they need me. And a newer world? I read these more painful essays and I wonder. Yet in these challenges are vestiges of hope like bright threads holding the world together, common threads that bind us close in this small room.*

Endnote

What sets worlds in motion is the interplay of differences, their attractions and repulsions. Life is plurality, death is uniformity. By suppressing differences and peculiarities, by eliminating different civilizations and cultures, progress weakens life and favors death. The ideal of a single civilization for everyone, implicit in the cult of progress and technique, impoverishes and mutilates us. Every view of the world that becomes extinct, every culture that disappears, diminishes a possibility of life.

—Octavio Paz
In *The Primal Mind*
by Jamake Highwater

Works Cited

Barth, Fredrik. *Ethnic Groups and Boundaries.* Boston: Little Brown, 1969.

Cassirer, Ernst. *An Essay on Man: An Introduction to a Philosophy of Human Culture.* Garden City, NY: Doubleday, 1953.

Curtis, N. *Indians' Book.* New York: Dover Publications, 1907.

Eliot, T. S. *Complete Poems and Plays 1909-1950.* "Little Gidding" from *Four Quartets.* New York: Harcourt, Brace, Jovanovich, 1971.

Fromm, Erich. *The Anatomy of Destructiveness.* New York: Ballantine, 1975.

_____. *The Revolution of Hope.* New York: Bantam Books, 1968.

Hammond, P. "Out of the Ashes." *CSUDH Alumni Digest* 1 (September 1992).

Highwater, Jamake. *The Primal Mind: Vision and Reality in Indian America.* New York: Penguin, 1981.

Huff, Delores J. "The Tribal Ethic: The Protestant Ethic and Economic Development." Contemporary American Indian Issues Series. University of California at Los Angeles: University of California Press, 1986.

Pico della Mirandola, Giovanni. Charles Glenn Wallace, translator. *On the Dignity of Man.* New York: Bobbs-Merrill, 1965.

Rieff, David. "The New Face of L.A." *Los Angeles Times* (15 September 1991).

Silko, Leslie Marmon. *Ceremony.* New York: Penguin Books, 1977.

Teilhard de Chardin, Pierre. *The Future of Man.* New York: Harper, 1959.

Tennyson, Alfred L. "Ulysses." In *The Selected Poetry of Tennyson,* edited by D. Bush. New York: Random House, 1951.

Tillich, Paul. *The Courage to Be.* New Haven: Yale University Press, 1952.

Warner, J. S., J. Hilliard, and V. Piro. *Visions across America.* New York: Harcourt, Brace, Jovanovich, 1992.

Whitman, Walt. *The Portable Walt Whitman.* New York: Viking, 1975.

Yevtushenko, Yevgeny. G. Reavey, translator/ed. *The Poetry of Yevgeny Yevtushenko, 1953 to 1965.* "Babii Yar." New York: October House, 1965.

DATE DUE

1-8-97			
MAR 1 7 1997			
SEP 0 5 2003			
GAYLORD			PRINTED IN U.S.A